AF316763

ALAN CRAWLEY AND *CONTEMPORARY VERSE*

ALAN CRAWLEY

AND

CONTEMPORARY VERSE

Joan McCullagh
with a foreword by Dorothy Livesay

UNIVERSITY OF BRITISH COLUMBIA PRESS
VANCOUVER

ALAN CRAWLEY AND *CONTEMPORARY VERSE*

This book has been published with the help of a grant from the Humanities Research Council of Canada using funds provided by the Canada Council and grants from The Hamber Foundation and The Leon and Thea Koerner Foundation.

Canadian Shared Cataloguing in Publication Data

McCullagh, Joan, 1932-
Alan Crawley and Contemporary Verse

A revision of the author's thesis, University of British Columbia.
Includes bibliography and index.
"Index to *Contemporary Verse* 1941-1952": p. 63
ISBN 0-7748-0047-X

1. Contemporary Verse. 2. Crawley, Alan. 3. Contemporary Verse—Indexes. I. Contemporary Verse. II. Title.
PS8001.C65M32 C811.5'05
PR9195.1.C

International Standard Book Number 0-7748-0047-X

Printed in Canada

Contents

Foreword

Here is a book that scarcely needs a foreward. It speaks for itself. Unlike most other critical appraisals of Canadian poets, the entire emphasis is on ''voice'': skillfully chosen excerpts from letters written to that most acute of listeners, the editor Alan Crawley. All I can do is commend Joan McCullagh's hard work and devotion not only in reading the correspondence to and from Crawley over eleven years, but in interviewing so many of the poets, in sending out questionnaires, in reading all their books! The excerpts chosen from letters now housed in the Douglas Library Archives, Queen's University, gain much by the author's perspicacity. Her desire has been to set down the controversial against the congenial, the critical against the laudatory. She succeeds admirably in giving life to the history of the rise and survival of the poetry quarterly *Contemporary Verse*. As well it is refreshing to find such a natural, unacademic approach to poets and poetry. They speak out here from the forties through their response to Alan Crawley as critic, friend, and editor. Canadian poetry may now be seen as a whole. It is likely to gain many devotees as a result of Joan McCullagh's research.

What I have to add to this picture, then, is peripheral. Having known Alan Crawley and his wife Jean intimately since 1938, it would seem appropriate for me to give others a glimpse of what they were like as people. Through those early years we lived near each other, he in West Vancouver and I in North Vancouver; so that rather than writing letters we talked on the telephone, we visited with each other every two or three weeks, we gave and received parties. Sometimes Jean would put Alan on a bus which I would meet. We would then enjoy the whole summer afternoon sitting out under the cherry tree until Jean or Michael, their younger son, called by for drinks and social laughter. Sometimes at night I made notes about our conversations, eventually to appear in articles or radio talks. And in later years there have been tape recordings of Alan reminiscing. Of these perhaps George Robertson's is the most vivid and technically pleasurable.[1] The man's voice cannot be shared by all, but his appearance and ambiance is clearly to be seen in the photograph by Murray Polson, taken in his eighty-fifth year. After a careful scrutiny of the long narrow face, the hawk-like Roman nose, the blind eyes still seeming alive as they look downward at a book, the high, thoughtful, furrowed forehead, the fine white hair, there emerges a Renaissance man, one who could have held forth with Shakespeare in a tavern or posed with Leonardo in a sunny Italian street. P.K. Page has suggested a Spanish aura: ''I remember this marvellously Spanish looking man. He looked as if he might have come out of an El Greco painting with this extraordinarily alive quality about him.'' Certainly Crawley's love of the sun would fit him well into a Mediterranean setting. Yet he seems never to have travelled there, and his boyhood was spent on the Manitoba prairie. The memory of sunshine and snow, black earth and blue sky sustained him even in his late eighties. ''How I'd love to visit Winnipeg again before I die!'' But if he had come he would not have been able to see it. Memory served him better.

His first memories were of his mother, Maude Buck, and of her gentle, serene influence. He was born on 23 August 1887, in the same house where she had been born at Coburg, Ontario. ''In my grandmother's house when I was a boy there were servants and an ordered way of life exactly parallel to that of an English country gentleman in England,'' says Crawley. So much for the myth that *Jalna* was not a true picture of pioneer upperclass life in Ontario in the 1890's. ''Of course it was!'' Nonetheless, a younger generation of Englishmen was coming out to Canada to seek something different. So it was with Charles James Crawley, a young bank clerk who went homesteading near Holland, Manitoba. Maude Buck had a sister here, married to another Englishman; so when she responded to pleas and came west, it was not surprising that she and Crawley met and became engaged. After their marriage the young couple travelled several times to England but ''could not stick it.'' So when the elder Crawley died they used his inheritance to return to Canada. It was on the way back to the prairies that Maude was obliged to stop off in her parents' home at Coburg to give birth to her third child (the first two had died in infancy). That third child was Alan. There was only one more to follow, Jack, some six years later.

Charles Crawley meanwhile bought a new farm, but rented it out in order to set up in business in Holland. His next move was to become a banker there; and eventually he sold his private bank to the Union Bank—with himself as manager. This was typical of the way banks developed on the prairies.

Although he grew up in a small town, Alan Crawley had a chance to roam through the surrounding rolling countryside. He remembered well his father's love of the outdoors, of riding and hunting, but he himself was not a sportsman, nor attracted to hunting. According to a school friend at St. John's College, Winnipeg, where Alan was sent as a boarder at the age of eight, the boy was never robust. He preferred piano playing to games. Books were his great joy, and it would seem that he had teachers at St. John's who encouraged his intellectual pursuits—as well as chastising him for his pranks. Those school years he though of as his happiest, because during that time he formed lifelong friendships. On some holidays he stayed with a schoolmate at Banff and experienced the challenge of mountain climbing.

One incident in his life at Holland when he was about age twelve may have had an unacknowledged but crucial influence on his later interests. It must have been during the Christmas season, and who should be coming to visit the tiny hamlet in a sleigh, covered with a buffalo robe, but the dramatic reader of her own poetry, Pauline Johnson! It seems she stayed with friends at the same house as young Crawley, and he was privileged to sit at her feet, stretched out on a bear rug by the fire, looking up at what was the most beautiful creature he had ever seen, or, indeed, might ever see. "We all trooped to the schoolhouse to hear her read. And there, of course, she wore the traditional Indian costume, and read her poems in a fine ringing voice." Although the young boy listening did not turn out to be a poet, that first-hand contact with a living writer may well have disposed him towards reading poetry for pleasure and saying it aloud.

Crawley once confided to me that he would have liked to become a journalist, but his parents, alarmed at the thought, insisted that the law was a much more secure direction to follow. So at seventeen he went straight from matriculation to law school. At that time, 1905, university courses were not prerequisite. Instead Crawley was articled. He was admitted to the bar in 1911 and then joined the firm of Machray, Sharpe, Dennistoun and Locke as a salaried member. Law students, like most professional men of the era, lived in boarding houses or took rooms together and hired housekeeping services. This convivial life was soon to be broken however with the declaration of war in August 1914. Most of Crawley's friends and his young brother went overseas immediately, but he was refused the A1 rating because of his weak eyesight. Instead he developed his skill in the profession. By the time he was twenty-eight he was well established, earning five hundred dollars a month, and much in demand socially. As one of his clients remembers, "Alan had a sparkling mind." It was during one of the wartime farewell parties that Crawely saw a fair, blue-eyed young woman descending the staircase. Then and there he said to himself, "That's the girl I'll marry." He did, in 1915.

Jean's people, the Horns, were of English-Scottish descent, and Jean had been sent from Winnipeg to a finishing school in England. Her father had come to Manitoba from Ottawa with the First Brigade (Riel Rebellion, 1885), and he stayed to become a well-known businessman in the Grain Exchange. The young people were supplied with a house near the river, and when their first son, David, was born in 1916 they were comfortable indeed with a cook, a servant, and a "nanny" for the nursery.

During the war Crawley had occasion to do some legal work in England. This gave him a fine opportunity to explore the historical and literary haunts of London. He told Joan McCullagh how one day during his rambles he stumbled upon Harold Munro's Poetry Bookshop, a landmark eagerly sought out by visiting poets such as Robert Frost. When Crawley went inside to get a taste of the feast, he found not only books, not only Harold Munro himself, but a meeting-place for poets who came to read their works aloud. This was a new experience for the young lawyer. In this way he became acquainted with the work of England's Georgian poets, Davies, Hodgson, de la Mare, as well as the war poets, Brooke, Owen, and Edward Thomas. Back in Canada Crawley kept in touch with Munro, ordering books of contemporary British poetry. He was not as yet reading any Canadian poetry, and in that era there was very little being published that would have been of interest to him. Roberts and Carman had been away from Canada for many years, and the younger experimentalists —W.W.E. Ross, Raymond Knister, and Louise Bowman—had not yet started to publish. Marjorie Pickthall was probably little known outside Toronto and Vancouver.

Winnipeg in the twenties was divided into two worlds. The cleavage occured in 1919 when the labour unions' call for a general strike was met by a rallying of the "Citizen's Committee of One Thousand." That story is now well known, but perhaps the most damning account of the unions' defeat can be found in the hysteria of newspaper accounts of the day.[2]

Ever since, Winnipeg has been divided between the haves and the have-nots, the Woodsworth followers versus the Grain Exchange, the fine luxurious brick houses along the Red and Assiniboine and the straggling, struggling, white clapboard immigrant cottages on the back streets. Although Alan Crawley was part and parcel of the upper crust world and a corporation lawyer himself, his respect for his profession and his strong sense of justice made him always an advocate for civil liberties. He might have gone far in the direction taken by Judge Stubbs had it not been for the catastrophe which hit Manitoba's social structure in 1932 and which perhaps led to his own illness. It was discovered that the trust funds of the University of Manitoba and of the Church of England were diverted by John Machray, the then chancellor of the university, into fraudulent speculations of his own. The result was a minor Watergate in Manitoba, best described by Arthur Lower in his autobiography *My First Seventy-Five Years:*

> Most of the difficulties in both University and College could be traced to poverty. The buildings of United College may have been shabby, but those of the University of Manitoba, while more extensive, were shabbier and dirtier. Staff salaries had been low even in the prosperous days, and when the depression came they sunk to abysmal levels. In 1932 the then chancellor and treasurer of the University was discovered to have invested University funds foolishly and later actually to have embezzled them. He was a nephew of a previous Archbishop of Rupert's Land, so American papers, not too nice in their distinctions, came out with flaring headlines declaring that "Archbishop Embezzles University's Funds." The Chancellor was a member of one of the old Red River families, which had held on in positions of influence long after the old colony had been submerged in the growing province. In that such families had "got in on

> the ground floor" and from their associations with the traditional institutions of the old fur-trading days, such as the Hudson's Bay Company and the Anglican Church, they are comparable with the Family Compact group of Upper Canada. Most provinces, in fact, have exhibited the same phenomenon. In Manitoba the embezzlement was to end it, suddenly and dramatically.[3]

One has a feeling that this was a blow from which Alan Crawley never recovered. He once told me he had never gone to church since the early thirties because he had found out that church-going Anglicans were as venal as anyone else. In this connection Crawley's very old friend, Supreme Court Judge C.H. Locke, Q.C. has recorded the following: "Alan was very much attached to John Machray who had been very kind to him and I am sure the discovery of the defalcations was a bitter blow." Judge Locke makes it abundantly clear that although in 1918 Machray and Sharpe were listed as being part of the firm with Locke, Parker and Crawley, changes came soon thereafter, with Locke, Parker, and Crawley setting themselves up as partners in the legal firm, whereas Machray and Sharpe carried on an investment practice. Alan was never employed by that firm...was not involved in any way in the defalcations... those occurred in the firm of Machray and Sharpe." Machray was tried and convicted and died in prison of cancer.

Crawley himself only once mentioned to me the events of 1932. "For two or three years I knew that in Machray's business something like this—diversion of funds—was going on, but there was nothing I could do. He kept re-investing other people's money." Beyond those remarks the matter has been a closed book. And indeed one who seeks to discuss those events with Manitobans is met with silence.

In 1933, following the scandals, the Crawleys were summering at Kenora when it became evident that Alan was experiencing trouble with his eyesight. He was found to have "chorditis," a not unusual disease caused by a virus. One dictionary explains: "Susceptible people are often in a run-down condition, in bad health. The disease may attack any part of the body." But in Crawley's case the disease attacked his eyes. In hopes of a cure, the family sent Alan to hospital in St. Paul for six months for fever treatment. One morning the doctor came in and said: "You're going home in a week." He replied, "That's fine! Am I going to be able to read again?" "No, you won't." "Then I don't care whether I ever go home."

That point, Crawley felt, was the lowest moment of his life. But the doctor took him up on his statement. If this were total *deafness*, he said, he could understand a man being in despair. "But blindness doesn't cut you off from social life, as deafness does. Make up your mind that you are going to live as before. You can do it, if you have the will." And before there was time to protest, the doctor had given him a walking stick and sent him to the bathroom alone. "Take a bath. And here's your shaving kit. Shave!" He did shave himself; standing in front of the mirror, pretending to see.

A woman friend who knew the Crawleys well at this time told the writer: "He had always worn glasses. . . . His eyes had always been weak but soon after the shock, when the virus attacked, it settled on the optical nerve endings. . . . Alan has told me that the pain was intense, for the first years—then, only when he became totally blind did the pain disappear." She remembered that even in his helplessness his sense of humour never deserted him: "You know," he said once, "Jean's friends seem to associate *blindness* with *deafness.* How they shout at me!" But it was both of the Crawley's enthusiasm and zest for life that pulled them through. "Alan never lived in an enclave. . . . There was absolutely no *snobisme* in his make-up, intellectual or social. People of all walks of life were his friends."

Speaking of his blindness, Crawley has commented: "Very few people know how hard a struggle it has been. Dependency is so hard to take. It is always with you. You can't fight it. I had always read every minute of the working day, therefore I had books to fall back on. Perhaps I had been building up a reserve all my life towards the present disaster. My wife, Jean, of course was wonderful and patient and understanding. She began by reading to me and when we came to Victoria in 1934 I began to learn braille. Two lessons were all I needed to begin working at it myself." Alan felt that his blindness had had good side effects. "It has made me much more tolerant and more sociable." I would say, however, that the enforced darkness simply brought to the fore Alan Crawley's innate sense of justice, honesty, impartiality, and his deep concern for other people's needs. Materially speaking, of course, it eliminated his wealth and status (in those days no one apparently considered that Crawley might have learned to cope and continue practising law as so many blind men have recently done). His blindness however provided him with leisure, and characteristically he prepared to make the best use possible of his interest in literature. His wife Jean preferred prose to poetry and would likely have read aloud only fiction and criticism had he not insisted on some poetry "so he could learn some things he loved by heart." Of course he first put them down in braille.

By the fall of 1934 when the family had moved to Victoria, Alan already had a repertoire of modern poetry which he recited aloud to friends. In January 1935, Mr. Bullock-Webster invited the ex-lawyer to attend a meeting at the Empress Hotel where modern American poetry was to be recited. At the conclusion, Mr. Crawley rose to his feet, "I cannot see," he remarked in his incisive, yet persuasive way, "that the poetry we have just heard is either typically American or typically modern. How about—." And here he went on to mention names of contemporary British poets (knowing less than nothing then, he explained, of Canadian ones). "After the meeting Doris Ferne came up and introduced herself and asked if I would come to a gathering to meet some local Canadian poets. She mentioned Floris McLaren and Anne Marriott."

So it turned out that as soon as Alan met these young Victoria poets he began to make a study of other contemporary Canadians. In Vancouver, where he moved the following year, he met Anne Angus who was doing reviews and criticism for the Vancouver press. She was so enchanted by his way of saying poetry that she arranged for readings at the Georgian Club and other Vancouver gatherings.

It was at about this time that I too moved to Vancouver, married there in 1937, and set up housekeeping in an apartment near Stanley Park. Alan Crawley, who kept a diary at that time, recorded our first meeting and our subsequent friendship:

> Later we moved to an apartment on the shores of English Bay near the Macnairs, and as I was once more able to get about a bit, Dorothy often walked with me and my cocker in Stanley Park. We talked of politics, conditions in Canada, social service work, of her youth and mine in the middle west, of the French Symbolists, of Eliot, Auden and Spender, and almost always, of her own writing and what she wanted to do with it.... That winter the sense of impending disaster to the world following the warning of the September appeasement was heavy. The Macnairs were distressed at many meetings with men who had returned to Canada after fighting such terrible odds against Fascism in Spain, and they had letters from friends still in that unhappy country....One afternoon, in an unusual sun, broken only occasionally by slashes of wind and rain, we sat together in Stanley Park. I repeated to Dorothy the magnificent "Spain" by W.H. Auden, lately read, that biting indictment of the past and present, and the sombre warning for the future:
>
> "Tomorrow, perhaps the future...
> The stars are dead; the animals will not look,
> We are left alone with our day, and the time
> is short and history to the
> defeated
> May say also but cannot help our pardon."
>
> The words sang over and over in our minds. On a nearby bench three men lounged dejectedly, shoulders slouched, heads down and legs outstretched. From time to time one of them got up to throw a stone into the water, and sat down again. Their voices in aimless talk came to us. Evidently they were killing the monotonous hours in idleness. "There,"

> said Dorothy, "there are the men who will have to fight for us when the time comes, the men we will ask to save our country and civilization which has done so little for them. I have seen them in Toronto, in Montreal and now in Vancouver and what am I doing to help them?"

Crawley concluded this part of his reminiscence with the following paragraph:

> During the spring of 1939 Dorothy and I worked together in presenting a series of poetry readings over a Vancouver radio network. One evening, after a radio broadcast we read the English translation of "Lament for a Dead Bullfighter," by Lorca, the Spanish poet, and the story of his life, the tragic execution and of the burning of his books in Barcelona, by Franco's mob. A few days later Dorothy read me her poem, LORCA.

In further comment Crawley told Charles Boylan "I was very much affected by it ['Lorca']. Later in my readings, I always said 'Lorca' was one of my favorite poems."

I have quoted these excerpts at some length to illustrate how totally committed Alan Crawley could be to another person and another person's work. Later letters from other poets testify to this wondergful gift. It followed naturally that in 1941 when four women poets met in Victoria to discuss the possibility of creating an avenue for poetry in little magazine format, there was no question as to who in Canada could best be its editor: "Alan Crawley!" I was designated to persuade him.

The rest of the story is well known. But perhaps what is less well known is Alan Crawley's view of his role as editor. I quote again from a taped interview by Charles Boylan:

> Since he had never attended University, Crawley explained that he had no pretensions as a literary critic. "I have never claimed that I could tell a person anything on the writing of poetry; I have never pretended to be a critic in a professional state at all. I've just simply said what I liked about poetry, the poems that I liked. If anyone asked me anything about it (over some years there were quite a number) I just tried to help them make the poems more acceptable, to stick to what they actually wanted to say. I've not any qualifications for telling people how to write poetry as in a creative writing class. I've never been a professor or teacher or anything of that kind."

In a taped interview I myself made an attempt to get Alan to set down his criteria. He was much against the academic exercise of tearing a poem apart for its imagery, or use of language, or structure, or tone. A poem appealed to him through his senses; and he used the analogy of his response to music to explain how he judged a poem. "I do not analyse Bach or Beethoven . . . I just let them speak to me and involve my feelings. But different kinds of music appeal. I'm not too fond of opera, but I respond to singing (lieder). I prefer piano music to strings; and of the moderns, much of Bartok delights me." He heard a poem in the same way, as a whole: first for its meaning; then for its clarity and precise choice of words, last for its rhythm and music. This led him to respond to a wide sweep of formal and informal poetry, objective and subjective; it tended to omit the narrative form. And if there is one area that left him uninterested, it was the long narrative poem, including much of Pratt. On the other hand, where narrative was juxtaposed with other dramatic or lyric material, as in Marriott's "Wind Our Enemy," Birney's "Trial of a City," or my own "Call My People Home," Crawley was genuinely enthusiastic.

What he could not abide was sentimentalism, loose or imprecise use of words, obscure metaphors, flat statement, useless adjectives. Indeed he sounded like Pound when he said (*a propos* of keeping abreast of the ideas and forms of the times):

> A poem isn't a picture. It's a statement of an idea. . . . Don't think that a description is a poem. And don't walk around your subject. Make your language like your speech. Be brief, clear-cut. Above all, cut out those descriptive adjectives.

Besides acting as a critic and as a talent scout for Canadian poetry, Alan Crawley was developing in those early war years the gift he had found when broadcasting in Winnipeg before his blindness set in: the gift of saying poetry aloud. He has been accused of "making poetry sound like prose." But he liked that accusation! "If the public doesn't like to have poetry read this way, with the emphasis on the meaning—then the public will have to be educated. Most poetry reading we hear nowadays, particularly on radio, drugs the listener. The emphasis is put on histrionics and rhythm." Alan Crawley's idea, on the contrary, was to make the idea in a poem come clean. Lazy people should not read poetry, said he.

Finally in an attempt to convey the "pure essence" of the man Crawley, it would be essential to hear his voice in the full vigour of those years when he was saying poetry aloud. Although one could trace in his voice the sound of generations behind him who had gone through the English Public School, nonetheless Alan Crawley spoke with a cool mellow "unaccent" shared by other public figures of that Canadian generation. Above all he hated histrionics, affected "Englishisms," or dressing up poetry in fancy clothes. He admitted that in the forties and fifties he was not always convinced that the poet was the best person to read his own work. Pratt's and Birney's readings did not please him. But he was deeply moved by Klein's sonorous fervour. "I heard him read to me in such a way as to emphasize his own passion and feeling." Klein, Crawley understood, was not an actor charging words with a manufactured rhetoric. And in listening to younger poets of the sixties Crawley conceded that they have learned how to read their own work aloud to bring out its power. The great pity is that Crawley's own interpretations were never recorded.

Yet there must be many in this country who have heard those incisive, confident tones, for in an arid time when poetry was the shabbiest of the arts Alan Crawley really did quicken the pulse for poetry in Canada. During and after the Second World War the editor was called upon to read to women's clubs and high schools in Vancouver and finally to tour Canada for the Canadian Club in 1946. From mid-October to late December he and his wife, having left Vancouver by boat to Prince Rupert, proceeded by the C.N.R. through Northern Alberta, Ontario, Quebec, and New Brunswick. On the way back they appeared at a number of smaller Ontario towns and cities. From Winnipeg they took the C.P.R. and wound their way back west through Saskatchewan, Alberta, and the Okanagan. For these one night stands Crawley was offering simply: "Contemporary Canadian Poetry." The response appears to have been exciting and rewarding for both the Crawleys and the communities. Crawley especially enjoyed meeting people in the remoter northern settlements. He became convinced, I believe, that poetry could become a part of the social life of the people.

In the fifties, after Crawley "folded" *Contemporary Verse*, the Crawleys had moved to the Okanagan, living near Penticton on a small fruit orchard. Their son Michael became a farmer for those few years, aided and abetted by the dynamic Jean Crawley until her heart attacks forced them to return to the coast. Finally the three of them settled at Cordova Bay, halfway between Victoria and Swartz Bay, an easy stopping place for visitors of all kinds—literary friends as well as bridge players and convivial friends from the Winnipeg era. Although formal in their pattern of social living and followers of a careful routine, Jean and Alan Crawley loved above all to have visitors for tea or drinks. And Crawley's "bevy of girls" (among whom one could name seven women poets) continued to write to him, to telephone, to visit whenever they were in the neighbourhood. Jean also delighted in these encounters, for she it was who was continuing to read aloud and keep Alan informed of all that would interest him. In the background Michael sat quietly, or went outside to weed his loganberry field, or came in to make tea or pour drinks. In 1970, when Jean was still alive and full of spirited interest in all his literary friendships, Alan wrote me in Edmonton what I took to be a sort of farewell testimonial. But it did not at that time, happily, mean farewell. I quote it only to show the extent of his capacity for generosity and love:

> May 3, 1970. . . . I feel confident that you are certain of my affection and the deep gratitude I can never lose for the aid and advice and encouragement that you were so generous with through the years when I was editing. And for the advice and help you have later given to both Jean and me. I feel that I am still carrying too much of the reticent English blood in me to express as I would like to do, the deepest of my feelings.

Although my friendship with Alan Crawley always remained platonic, in the time of my need I was truly in love with this man (as my poem "Nocturne" testifies). He in his old age (and in his cups!) confided that he had also been in love with me. We sustained each other through some darker years, yet remained loyal to our enjoined commitments. I think there were other women who loved him, and they loved Jean also. The pair were indivisible: Jean the party-loving socialite who had to give up that way of life when her husband became blind, but a woman with a keen mind and a great interest in contemporary literature and the Canadian political scene; Alan the more meditative yet perhaps with a greater commitment to politics and social reconstruction. Both were open to philosophical discourse and had a deep interest in Buddhism and the eastern interpretation of man's place in the universe. Jean Crawley died quietly at Eastertime, 1971, leaving the lives of Alan and Michael so thoughtfully planned that they continued to live in the house on Sayward Road as if Jean were still with them.

If I were asked for a final word to say about Alan Crawley as friend it would be this: his concern for women—so often bound to the mundane role in their daily lives—his concern was immense and intense. Although blind, he gladly did dishes, ran the washing machine, brought in wood for the fireplace—the chores of drudgery which he thought women were endlessly committed to in his day and age. He longed as much as we did that women should have time to themselves, time to create. It was this that made him a tower where sometimes we could come and lean and obtain strength.

Dorothy Livesay

Acknowledgements

For permission to quote from personal correspondence, the author is grateful to Dorothy Livesay, Jay Macpherson, P.K. Page, Jack McClelland, Earle Birney, Audrey Sutherland, Raymond Souster, James Reaney, Daryl Hine, Beth Pierce Robinson, A.J.M. Smith, Sandor Klein, Irving Layton, Louis Dudek, Roy Daniells, Lillian Stevenson Pollock, F.R. Scott, Margaret Avison, and Desmond Pacey.

Abbreviations

Personal correspondence is used extensively in this work; the following abbreviations are used to refer to holders of this correspondence in the internal documentation.

AC	Alan Crawley
JMcC	Joan McCullagh
FMcL	Floris Clark McLaren
JM	Jay Macpherson
UT	University of Toronto

(The bulk of the correspondence described in this book as held by Alan Crawley was transferred to Queen's University subsequent to this book's being completed.) Where the date of a letter is not indicated in the text, it is supplied.

Introduction

"It all began in 1925 in the environs of McGill University," wrote Louis Dudek and Michael Gnarowski in *The Making of Modern Poetry in Canada.*[1] "To the envy of less happy cities. . . ," Dudek said elsewhere, "one of the particularities in the development of English poetry in Canada over the past thirty years has been the dominant role of Montreal as a center of activity and a source of new poetry."[2] In "Patterns of Recent Canadian Poetry," he took a wider look but arrived at the same conclusion: "From 1927 (Scott's and Smith's beginning) to 1949 (the date of Reaney's 'The Red Heart'), the modern movement was almost entirely centered in Montreal. . . . There may be no 'school' in Montreal; but the poets of Montreal seem to share a few principles on the social direction and on the experimental direction—toward natural speech—of modern poetry; and in this they must inevitably provide the central drive to the national literature in its movement away from nineteenth century modes."[3] Munro Beattie agreed in the *Literary History of Canada*. "In the history of twentieth-century Canadian poetry two Montreal publications (the *McGill Fortnightly Review* and *Canadian Mercury*) are documents of peculiar importance. . . . The aims of the young editors and contributors were both critical and creative. . . . They would be, these young critics and poets of Montreal, the importers of new influences, and they would demonstrate in their own writings how the new influences might reinvigorate Canadian poetry."[4] Later on, discussing the "renaissance" of the forties and the little magazines *Preview* and *First Statement*, Beattie referred to Montreal as "still headquarters for the modern movement in Canadian poetry."[5]

Desmond Pacey was less categorical in *Creative Writing in Canada*. He mentioned other poets from other places—Dorothy Livesay, Earle Birney, W.W.E. Ross, Raymond Knister—and worried that "the actual creative performance of the whole group of Montreal poets has been less than might have been expected."[6] Still, his summation followed the general trend:

> The thirty years from 1920 to 1950, then, saw much activity in Canadian poetry. The emergence of E.J. Pratt and of the Montreal School in the twenties marked the beginning of the modernist movement; in the thirties there was a slackening caused largely by the depression and the difficulty of finding publication; but in the forties Pratt and Montrealers were joined by a whole host of new poets. Never before had there been so many interesting poets writing in Canada at a time.[7]

Peter Stevens's *The McGill Movement* is further evidence of the dominant role assigned to the Montreal Group in the development of modern poetry in Canada.

No one would seriously argue with the important part eastern writers and publications have played in naturalizing modernism in Canada. One agrees with Earle Birney that though the *McGill Fortnightly Review* was "short-lived, it yet existed long enough to launch some of the best poets to write in Canada in this century, and eventually to influence, by stimulus or reaction, most of what poetry has succeeded it in the country";[8] and with Wynne Francis who said that "the tension set up between [*Preview* and *First Statement*] generated much of the poetic activity that went on in Montreal and made the 'Forties Canada's most exciting literary decade."[9] However, this approach oversimplifies the course of modern poetry in Canada and ignores the important part played by writers and publications from places other than Montreal (and Toronto). In the forties much of the best poetry being written was consistently recognized and published, not by *Preview* and *First Statement* in the east, but by *Contemporary Verse* in the west, and the exclusion of Alan Crawley's *Contemporary Verse* from serious study has resulted in a distortion of the development of Canadian poetry during the forties.

Even serious students of Canadian literature may not know Alan Crawley's little west coast magazine *Contemporary Verse*, although it ran for more than eleven years. There are polite, usually respectful references to it in the literary histories. Desmond Pacey was complimentary in *Creative Writing in Canada*: "Alan Crawley founded *Contemporary Verse* in 1941 with the specific object of encouraging the new poetry in Canada, and showed almost impeccable taste in the choice of good poetry and in providing sympathetic and perceptive reviews of the current output of verse."[10] (Pacey worried that Crawley might miss the tribute and wrote to him on 25 June 1952, "I hope you noticed the brief and inadequate but very sincere tribute I paid you and your magazine?")[11] Munro Beattie was more generous, devoting a full paragraph to Crawley and his magazine in the *Literary History of Canada*. He called Crawley a "gifted editor" and said, "To read through the files of this small, neat magazine, is to feel sustained respect for Mr. Crawley's judgment and catholicity, and astonishment at the number of good Canadian poets who sent him their poems."[12] *Contemporary Verse* fared less well in Dudek and Gnarowski's highly regarded *The Making of Modern Poetry in Canada*. Raymond Souster is quoted as saying to Dudek, "I think you're probably as fed up with *Contemporary Verse* and *Northern Review* as I am, and I know there are plenty of others who feel the same way";[13] and in their discussion of little magazines, the authors relegate *Contemporary Verse* to the "largest category" of little magazines—"the uncommitted or eclectic magazines."[14] Dudek was more specific in his article "The Role of Little Magazines in Canada," but the deprecatory tone is still present. Crawley was "handicapped by blindness and cornered in the far west," Dudek said, and he condemned *Contemporary Verse* for not being a fighting magazine with a policy":

> It was concerned only with publishing "good poetry"—which, in itself, can embody an affirmation—but it did not in addition work out any program of ideas which this poetry could fire. It lasted for ten years, however, carrying sparks from any source which might show a flicker in that period.[15]

A few articles have been written about the magazine including Floris McLaren's "Contemporary Verse: A Canadian Quarterly" in *Tamarack Review* but few people know them.[16] *Canadian Literature* published two articles avowing the importance of Crawley and his magazine to modern poetry—Ethel Wilson's article "Of Alan Crawley" in 1964[17] ,and George Robertson's documentary "Alan Crawley and Contemporary Verse" in 1969.[18] These articles made Alan Crawley a little better known, but they did not explore the significant contribution *Contemporary Verse* made to poetry during the forties. In spite of the fact that Alan Crawley edited the first modern poetry magazine in Canada and continued it thoughout the decade of the forties, set and maintained the high standards essential for the growth of new poetry, and was influentially involved with a number of major poets of the period, he and *Contemporary Verse* have been largely ignored by the critics. The development of modern poetry in Canada is usually presented as an eastern and, even more specifically, a Montreal accomplishment. Modernism in poetry supposedly began in the twenties in Montreal with the "Montreal Group," developed steadily to become "the dominant mood of Canadian poetry" by 1936 with the publication of *New Provinces*,[19] and was finally tempered by the conflict between the two Montreal little magazines *Preview* and *First Statement* in the early forties.

But was modern poetry really "the dominant mood of Canadian poetry" by 1936? Critics seem unanimous in their opinion that modern poetry was firmly established by the mid-thirties, but there is scant evidence to support their conclusion. Of the dozens of books of poetry published in the decade, the majority are patently not modern. Audrey Alexandra Brown, Mary E. Colman, Charles G.D. Roberts, Carol Coates, A.M. Stephen, Edna Jaques, Gordon LeClaire, Watson Kirkconnell, Robert Service, Arthur S. Bourinot, A.G. Bailey, Charles Bruce, Kenneth Leslie, Wilson MacDonald, Duncan Campbell Scott, Floris Clark McLaren, Leo Cox, Alan Creighton, and Ralph Gustafson (this list is not complete) all had at least one volume of poetry published, and several had more than one. In addition, annual yearbooks of non-modern poetry from various branches of the Canadian Authors' Association continued to be published through the Depression, and a number of very traditional anthologies appeared to supplement W. Garvin's 1926 *Canadian Poets* and A.M. Stephen's *Golden Treasury of Canadian Verse* of 1928.

By contrast, little modern poetry was published during the thirties—certainly not enough to support the claim that modernism was the "dominant mood" at that time. There were *New Provinces*, three collections from E.J. Pratt, Dorothy Livesay's *Signpost* (1932), W.W.E. Ross's *Laconics* (1930) and *Sonnets* (1932), Leo Kennedy's *The Shrouding* (1933), L.A. MacKay's *Viper Bugloss* (1938), Anne Marriott's chapbook *The Wind Our Enemy* (1939). And in these collections the modernism is tentative and uncertain.

Periodicals, generally a more sensitive indicator of new trends than other forms of publication, were remarkably unadventurous in the thirties and early forties. After the two early periodicals which were directly involved with the beginnings of the Montreal movement (the *McGill Fortnightly Review*, November 1925-April 1927, and *Canadian Mercury*, 1928-1929), no other journal favoured the work of moderns until the equally short-lived *New Frontier* of 1936-1937, which was primarily interested in left-wing, social realism poetry. *Canadian Forum* maintained a liberal policy toward modern poetry, but traditional poetry preponderates in most issues. After its promising beginning in 1936 (Dorothy Livesay's "Day and Night" was featured, and F.R. Scott, Finch, Kennedy, and Anne Marriott were represented), *Canadian Poetry Magazine* quickly settled into mediocrity as the official organ of the Canadian Authors' Association.

The critical opinion that modern poetry was established in Canada by the mid-thirties seems to be based largely on the evidence of *New Provinces*. But when this small volume of poetry was published in 1936 *New Provinces* was not the manifestation of a viable modern poetry movement, as the Montreal group realized. It was very much an after-the-fact publication. F.R. Scott wrote in the preface that the poems in the collection "were written for the most part when new techniques were on trial, and when the need for a new direction was more apparent than the knowledge of what that direction would be."[20] The brand of modernism produced by the Montreal group was largely derived from Yeats and Eliot—an exciting antidote to the excesses and irrelevancies of romanticism in the twenties, but quickly rendered obsolete by cultural changes and new trends in British and American poetry in the thirties.

A.J.M. Smith also felt that "a large number of verses in this book were written at a time when the contributors were inclined to dwell too exclusively on the fact that the chief thing wrong with Canadian poetry was its conventional and insensitive technique. Consequently, we sometimes thought we had produced a good poem when all we had done in reality was not produce a conventional one."[21] Smith agreed with Scott that new directions must be found for poetry in Canada in 1936. Detachment and self-absorption are becoming impossible, Smith wrote, "the artist who is concerned with the most intense of experiences must be concerned with the world situation." The poet "must try to perfect a technique that will combine power with simplicity and sympathy with intelligence so that he may play his part in developing mental and emotional attitudes that will facilitate the creation of a more practical social system." But in 1936 there was in Canada "only the faintest foreshadowing" of poetry such as this.[22]

In his unpublished dissertation, "The Development of Canadian Poetry between the Wars and Its Reflection of Social Awareness," Peter Stevens commented that "Canadian poets of the 1930's were faced with two almost insuperable problems: firstly, there was no real audience for modern poetry; secondly, there was no cohesive intellectual core of political thinking."[23] It must have seemed a new low for proponents of modernism in 1936 when *Canadian Poetry Magazine* began, for this journal had the distinction of being Canada's only poetry magazine, and it was controlled by the Canadian Authors' Association. "We believe," editor E.J. Pratt wrote in the second number, "that the long-established modes are far from their point of exhaustion and are everywhere giving evidence of fresh vision and vitality."[24] In the June 1936 issue of *New Frontier* Leo Kennedy's frustrated outburst, "Direction for Canadian Poets," suggested that modernism had a long way to go. Turning his back on his own "Shrouding" poetry along with that of the rest of the Montreal group, Kennedy insisted that "we need poetry that reflects the lives of our people, working, loving, fighting, groping for clarity. We need satire—fierce, scorching, aimed at the abuses which are destroying our culture and which threaten life itself."[25]

"There is a placid flatness to the run of Canadian poetry whether of 1882 or 1936 which invokes a smile of tolerance from the uninvolved observer, and makes the concerned participant—who looks for the work of adult minds—to squirm and suffer at so much documented obeisance to the namby-pamby," Kennedy went on.

> Changes have taken place in modern English poetry; the United States has experienced a sequence of upheavals since the first crusading days of Harriet Monroe. In England and in the States those younger poets with anything to say have forced their way out of the back-water of the '20's. They have analysed the forces making for social disintegration, and have allied themselves with the progressive movement that offers freedom of function and hope of life. Reading Canadian poetry, you would hardly suspect this.[26]

Scott had hoped, in his *New Provinces* preface, that the Depression might give some guidance to poets:

> In confronting the world with the need to restore order out of social chaos, the economic depression has released human energies by giving them positive direction. The poet today shares in this release, and contemporary English and American verse as a consequence shows signs of regaining the vitality it had lost.[27]

But it had not. Knister was dead, and even before his death he had turned most of his energies to prose; and W.W.E. Ross did not noticeably alter his imagist verse as a result of the Depression. The poetic output of A.J.M. Smith, Robert Finch, and Leo Kennedy sharply declined during the thirties, and all of these poets left Canada. Scott's satiric jabs at the faults and weaknesses of society had begun before the Depression and remained his most characteristic voice during this period. Pratt continued to develop his individual, primarily religious and narrative, style apart from the mainstream of Canadian poetry. Even in his shorter poems where he explores social themes, Pratt's orientation is essentially religious—seeing man's suffering in terms of his own sin or fault—rather than political or economic.

Dorothy Livesay and A.M. Klein did change direction as a result of the social situation of the thirties; although with Klein, whose chief impetus and sustaining vitality came from the Jewish tradition, it was more of an enrichment—a new theme to explore—rather than an actual redirection. Livesay gave up writing poetry entirely for a brief time after her 1932 *Signpost* collection; then reappeared in new proletarian dress in the mid-thirties with such poems as "Day and Night" and "The Outrider." She wrote more personal, lyric poems of social realism as well, obviously influenced by the work of Auden and his group, published in such magazines as *Canadian Poetry Magazine*, *Canadian Forum*, and *New Frontier*. Earle Birney had been on the literary scene in Canada since the mid-thirties—he was an editor of *Canadian Forum* from 1936 to 1940—but he did not write poetry in any amount until the forties.

Modern poetry had the techniques and the idiom to reflect and to interpret man's situation in the contemporary world, but the right combination of these elements for Canada was slow in evolving. Neo-metaphysical poetry, which had been so influential in the twenties with the Montreal group, did not have the same relevance to the thirties and forties. Its complexity and intellectual quality, which had seemed such an exhilarating antidote to the excesses of romanticism in the twenties, now seemed too cerebral and difficult, too aloof and cold. In 1936 W.E. Collin recognized this in *The White Savannahs* where he wrote: "Although the newer poets were brought up under Eliot, he can no longer lead them. The economic and social realities of life have hounded them, driven them to bay and they have had to face them."[28] Imagist poetry which probed with such clarity, simplicity, and precision into the "thingness" of things was limited by its very aims: it did not interpret; it did not comment; it did not inspire men to action. It simply did not say enough to a people struggling to cope with massive social disorder. Conversely, proletarian poetry—such as Livesay's "Day and Night"—spoke too obviously and too didactically. Inspired by Marxist and humanitarian ideals and anxious to right the injustices of an unjust society, this poetry too often lapsed into overt moralizing, exhortation, and propaganda. Auden, Spender, MacNeice, and (to a lesser extent) Dylan Thomas were revitalizing poetry in England and the United States during the thirties. Their influences did not really filter through to Canada until the forties.

Except for a few of Dorothy Livesay's poems, some from the Montreal group, the work of W.W.E. Ross, and the original voice of E.J. Pratt, Canadian poetry before the Second World War was essentially derivative. In a long letter to the Editors of *New Frontier* in October 1936, Alan Calmer (an American critic) confronted Canadian poets thus:

> I get the feeling from *New Provinces* and *The White Savannahs* that you have been largely content to take over these transformations in American and English verse at their face value, without rooting them very deeply in your own native patterns. It seems to me that you have not dug into the varied meanings and shades of meanings which these new tendencies must have for Canadian poetry alone, or the particular relevance which Canadian poetry must have to these new ways of writing. My impression is that you have welcomed these new attitudes in an altogether uncritical fashion, that you have been inflexible and unthinking, and even smug, towards them—that you have not hammered away at them, gripping them with all your might, squeezing out of them the sustenance which your poetic growth requires. I feel that you have adopted the modes of literary expression almost as meekly and blindly as your predecessors imitated the tones and moods of English Romantic poetry.[29]

At the end of the decade E.J. Pratt and A.J.M. Smith assessed the situation of Canadian poetry for the *University of Toronto Quarterly*, and it is obvious that modernism is anything but ascendent. Pratt tried to keep on the good side of both traditionalists and modernists with a middle-of-the-road article: "Tradition and revolt are inevitable complements like rain and sun: the first by itself mildews; the second burns or explodes. . . . Excellent work is done by writers following the liberal tradition," Pratt wrote, and "a group of young writers relatively small in numbers, but compensating by their intensity of conviction and by their study of experimental forms, are infusing new energy into our literature."[30] In his discussion Smith was still touting as "our best poetry" the early thirties' poetry of Kennedy, Livesay, Ross, and Pratt, supplemented by "careful craftsmen, such as F.O. Call, Leo Cox, Arthur S. Bourinot, and A.M. Stephen" and poems "here and there in the files of the *Canadian Forum*."[31]

In 1941, E.K. Brown was invited to edit a special Canadian number for *Poetry* (Chicago) and to prepare a critical and historical summary to accompany his selection of poems. The thirty poems that Brown chose as the best current Canadian work were from the *New Provinces* writers, and also Dorothy Livesay, D.C. Scott, Floris Clark McLaren, Mary Elizabeth Colman, L.A. MacKay, Louise Morey Bowman, and Anne Marriott. He concluded his analysis ("The Development of Poetry in Canada, 1880-1940") by stating that the "more conservative strains have been abundantly represented in the poetry of the past twenty years: a glance through the best anthology of recent Canadian verse, Mrs. Ethel Hume Bennett's *New Harvesting* (1939), will show that the majority of competent verse-writers in Canada have been little affected by the movement which began with the *McGill Fortnightly*."[32]

This, then, was the situation of poetry in Canada in the early forties when Alan Crawley started *Contemporary Verse*. Modernism had been introduced to Canada in the twenties, but it was essentially grafted stock that bore little fruit in the thirties when the whole cultural climate changed. New roots were needed, new shoots that could produce a tough, socially relevant, indigenous poetry. The first sign of this new growth in Canadian poetry was the appearance of Alan Crawley's little magazine in the fall of 1941. For the next decade Crawley and *Contemporary Verse* were significantly involved with the development of modern poetry in Canada.

It is my purpose here to make the contents of *Contemporary Verse* more accessible and better known by means of an index and to explore the contribution that Alan Crawley made to the development of modern poetry in Canada by editing *Contemporary Verse* (1941-1952), by criticizing and counselling poets, and by generally fostering an interest in poetry through lectures, radio talks, and poetry-reading tours. As much as possible Crawley and his contemporaries speak for themselves through their letters.

CHAPTER ONE

Contemporary Verse: Beginnings

In the early forties a surge of poetic activity followed the bleak thirties. ''Perhaps there never was a time in Canada when so many poets of promise appeared simultaneously or when...there was so much creative variety, as in the early forties,'' John Sutherland wrote in 1951 in ''The Past Decade in Canadian Poetry.'' ''The phenomenal development of Canada during the last war...gave a marked impetus to poetry as it did to the arts generally. There was an excitement in the air to which no one—least of all the poet—could fail to respond.''[1] Three little magazines devoted exclusively to modern work along with Earle Birney's *David and Other Poems*, Ralph Gustafson's *Anthology of Canadian Poetry* and *Little Anthology of Canadian Poets*, and A.J.M. Smith's *Book of Canadian Poetry* and *News of the Phoenix* appeared between 1941 and 1943. Before the war ended A.M. Klein, Dorothy Livesay, F.R. Scott, Patrick Anderson, Miriam Waddington, and Irving Layton had first books published, and Birney a second, *Now is Time*; two more magazines, *Direction* and *Northern Review*, and the anthology *Unit of Five* had appeared. Canadian poetry had entered a new phase—the ''Renaissance of the Forties.''

Chronologically it began with *Contemporary Verse*. ''I date the beginning of this decade from the first publication of *Contemporary Verse* in 1941,'' John Sutherland wrote:

> Many of the poets who appeared during the forties were introduced in the early issues of that magazine. Shortly afterwards, some of the same writers came together in Montreal and began producing publications of their own—*Preview* and *First Statement*,...—but *Contemporary Verse* had already stolen part of their thunder, and it deserves the first credit.[2]

The first issue of *Contemporary Verse*, small, thin, and unpretentious, was delivered to a handful of subscribers and a few indulgent newsstands in October 1941. It contained fourteen lithographed pages, nine poems, and a brief foreword by the editor explaining its purpose. Alan Crawley said:

> Conviction was added to my belief that beauty and truth is not all-told; that there are many writers of our own times who can speak to us in words and images and forms that interest and appeal; and that, for most of us, their writings are too hard to come by. A small group of readers and writers, sharing these feelings, send out this first issue of CONTEMPORARY VERSE, A CANADIAN QUARTERLY, in high hope that it and succeeding numbers may play a worthy part in the building of Canadian literature. (1:2) [3]

The issue has a strong early forties' flavour. Not all the poems can be termed modern, and the majority have a rawness about them that is characteristic of this transition period. All of the poems deal with the real world and man's situation in it, and in this sense they are modern; but they are uneven in quality. There is an attempt at informal language and natural speech rhythms, and at uncomplicated, realistic imagery; but sentimental traditionalism and self-consciousness hover around the edges of the poems. Western writers dominate, and the members of the founding committee each have a poem in this first issue. Earle Birney, P.K. Page, Floris McLaren, Leo Kennedy, Dorothy Livesay, A.J.M. Smith, Doris Ferne, and Anne Marriott are the contributors. This regional, small-group aspect of the first issue made Crawley a little uneasy, and subsequent numbers of the magazine have a broader representation. Some of the poems in the first issue are not new work—Smith's "The Face," Livesay's "The Child Looks Out," and, one suspects, Kennedy's "Carol For Two Swans"—which suggests that modern poets had a scanty store of poems for publication that summer of 1941. It was a quiet beginning for Canada's first modern poetry magazine but noisy enough to be heard across Canada. In a review which also considered *Preview* and *First Statement*, P.K. Page, a Previewer, stated just that: "The first—Contemporary Verse—did not say a particular loud 'boo' to the pink tea pretties but it was loud enough for one of their wags to dub it Contemptible Verse in a moment of irritation. That was possibly its first real victory." [4]

The real beginnings of *Contemporary Verse* antedated this first issue by several months. "The beginning was in the best tradition: enthusiastic, unpremeditated, and by any standards except those of little magazine publication, wildly unbusinesslike," Floris McLaren reminisced in a *Tamarack Review* article in 1957. [5] When Dorothy Livesay was visiting Floris McLaren in the spring of 1941 in Victoria, they talked of starting a modern poetry magazine. The need was there: "The chances of publication in Canada for an unknown writer, or for a writer experimenting with new verse forms, or concerned with social or political themes, were almost non-existent," McLaren wrote. "In England and the United States small literary magazines sprouted freely, welcoming new writers, encouraging fresh techniques, fighting vigorous battles with the mass-guardianship of public taste. They had in 1941 no relatives in Canada."[6] Dorothy Livesay had been an editor of *New Frontier* and knew a little about magazines, and Doris Ferne and Anne Marriott were willing to help. Dorothy Livesay was the most active and the most modern of the four, but the others were serious and enthusiastic about poetry. E.K. Brown praised the work of such west coast poets in "Letters in Canada: 1941." "An astonishing number of the most original and accomplished of the younger Canadian poets are in British Columbia, and among the most promising in this collection [*Victoria Poetry Chapbook*] are the poems of Miss Anne Marriott, Miss Doris Ferne, Mrs. Floris Clark McLaren, and Miss Pauline Howard."[7] Still it seemed a risky venture. "We poked tentatively at the edges of the idea and it began to seem possible," McLaren remembered. They decided to try. To avoid "the inevitable compromises" of an editorial board and give the magazine "a personal life and flavour," the founding committee decided to ask Alan Crawley to act as editor.[8]

Crawley was well qualified to edit a modern poetry magazine, for he had been a student of contemporary poetry since a chance meeting with Harold Munro in Munro's Poetry Book Shop in London in 1917, a meeting he described in a few notes put together as a "Personal History." "Mr. Munro was alone at that time and finding I was a Canadian talked to me for some time and questioned me on my reading and interest in writers, and after an hour or so of this friendly chat made me think that I could find a new interest in the Georgian poets and the young war poets and I came away with three books, the first books of poetry I had ever bought." Crawley was so taken with this poetry that he returned to the Poetry Book Shop for more poetry and more talk. "I was so interested with these and in other talks with Mr. Munro and the hearings of poets, Hodgson, de la Mare, Davies and others I had the good chance to hear that my interest in English poetry and especially in its reading aloud has grown and continued" (AC). From 1917 Crawley collected books of poetry and formed the habit of reading a poem each day and memorizing many of them. It was through this habit that he collected his phenomenal storehouse of sounds, rhythms, moods, and images which were the basis of what Desmond Pacey called his "almost impeccable taste." During the twenties and first few years of the thirties Crawley gave a series of talks on poetry in Winnipeg (some of them broadcast), a practice he continued when he moved to the west coast in 1934.

Alan Crawley saw the need for a liberal, intelligent, modern poetry magazine in Canada, and he had the time and the enthusiasm to edit such a magazine. But there were problems. Alan Crawley was blind and he lived in Caulfeild (now part of West Vancouver); Floris McLaren, who had agreed to the heavy job of publication and business manager, lived in Victoria. Crawley could manage informal correspondence, but more official letters required greater typing accuracy than he had. Manuscripts would have to be read several times until Crawley had memorized them or typed them into braille for his future reference. Dorothy Livesay in Vancouver could help a little, but her time was limited by her young family and her own writing. Obviously, the bulk of this kind of work would fall to Jean Crawley, Alan's wife, who was also a busy housewife and not particularly interested in poetry. Finances were bound to create problems too. *Canadian Poetry Magazine* was in continual financial difficulty in spite of the support of the Canadian Authors' Association, and modern poetry could claim even fewer readers. In fact, with the war in its second year and the outlook for the Allies anything but favourable, would anyone read poetry at all? But, most problematic of all, was enough modern poetry being written in Canada to warrant a magazine devoted exclusively to such work?

Alan Crawley made his decision, and on Tuesday, 3 June 1941, wrote to the committee members in Victoria, "to the conspirators" who "started all this":

> In spite of the distress of the times and the prospect of continued disquiet and unsettled days to come, I feel that the idea of the publication of a magazine of Canadian Poetry is a worthwhile and reasonable venture that could if properly managed and edited do much to help modern Canadian writers for I know of no publication that is now giving this possible help to writers. I am willing and enthusiastic to do what I can for it.

The decision once made, the magazine took shape. Crawley proposed a working arrangement which was accepted by the committee. The board of founders—Alan Crawley, Floris McLaren, Dorothy Livesay, Anne Marriott, and Doris Ferne—would decide matters of policy and management; the editor would read all manuscripts submitted and "have the sole right of rejection or acceptance," and he would determine the content, the arrangement of material, and the "policy of type of material of each issue. . . . This would not of course mean," Crawley added, "that I would not take part in any discussion and be ruled by majority decision on policy of magazine as a whole" (FMcL). As it worked out, there were no disputes either over policy or selection of poems during the course of the magazine. From the first issue to the last, it was Alan Crawley's journal. A name was decided upon: *Contemporary Verse: A Canadian Quarterly.* Some members of the founding committee felt that manuscripts from outside of Canada should not be accepted but in Crawley's mind the designation "Canadian" simply indicated that the magazine was a

Canadian venture. He wrote to Dorothy Livesay after the second number was out:

> Re "Canadian" as I wrote you I do completely disagree with Sedgewick that Canadian in subtitle suggests limitation. The three in Victoria are a bit wavery about taking MSS from outside Canada and left it pretty much to my editorial judgement. Already we have used work by Kennedy, Smith and Gustafson all in U.S.A. and I have accepted several MSS for future numbers from writers in U.S.A. (AC, nd)

"A magazine, once established, sets up a sort of magnetic field; like attracts like, and writers find their way to it, but the first numbers must set the pattern."[9] The immediate problem facing Crawley was finding good copy for the first issue of *Contemporary Verse*. Perhaps offering a gentle hint to the founding members, Crawley wrote in his letter accepting the editorship: "I am most anxious that this should not be a boost to friends of the founders and certainly not a magazine of work by a small group." If the magazine were to have any real value, high standards must be set and maintained. Crawley discussed this with Floris McLaren in a later letter:

> I do truly feel that after so many years of study and trying to understand I know something about writing and poetry in particular and that I have something to offer in my line of appreciation and criticism and I do not want to let that go or to release any of my standards and that if C.V. is to have to be just another channel for middle class and the lesser verse then we are wasting time which could be much better used. (FMcL, Oct. 1941)

"We could count on work from British Columbia," McLaren stated, "but we felt that it was important that the magazine...should not begin as a regional publication."[10] To avoid this, Crawley and Livesay wrote directly to poets across Canada asking for work. P.K. Page was one of the poets solicited, and many years later she described in *Canadian Literature* her reaction to Crawley's request:

> I was living in New Brunswick at the time...and had had very little published. And then this letter arrived...would I be prepared to send in something for Volume One of *Contemporary Verse*. This was a very revolutionary sort of thing to happen because...there weren't poetry magazines much in those days—this was the dim dark ages...and certainly nobody ever asked you for a poem. So this was quite exciting.[11]

As the September deadline for the first issue approached, Crawley had serious doubts about the quality of the poetry he had accepted; so little poetry had been submitted that he wondered if there were modern poets in Canada. He confided his concern to Floris McLaren:

> Also take it from the letter you are not so discouraged by the MSS in hand as I was and still sneakingly at times still am. How I should have liked to have so much and such good stuff that I was raring to go and just could not keep the things to myself and had to print them but that bunch may come and in the meantime I shall keep most of my pessimism and let it be tempered with optimism and hope as my temperament will allow. (FMcL, Sept. 1941)

Cheered by her optimistic reply and determined to make a beginning, even though the copy disappointed him, Crawley sent his selection of poems for *Contemporary Verse* 1 to Victoria for printing. One hundred copies were made in late September and seventy-five were mailed to subscribers in the first week of October 1941. Now, sounding much more assured with a copy of the magazine actually in hand, Crawley wrote to McLaren:

> First so many thanks for your letter which came Saturday and bucked me no end, that and Anne Marriott's equally cheering and heartening letter of the same mail helped me a great deal for I was being chicken hearted about the whole thing and especially of my ability to do what was expected of me. Now I feel the sword is unsheathed once more and I am able to at least hold and brandish it even if the thrusts are timid and unconvincing. What I said in the foreword was not idle chatter on my part and I still think there is good stuff if we can find and get it. That is the job just now. We seem to have made a fine start and with interest and subscribers and so it is up to us. (FMcL, Sept. 1941)

Reaction to *Contemporary Verse* 1 was immediate. In a letter to Crawley, Earle Birney was enthusiastic but not uncritical:

> Kennedy's "carol" is as finished as anything he's done and gave a necessary light-relief to the issue, and Dorothy Livesay's is a fine piece of imagination, which shows how to be "tight" without being knotted. I can't say the same for Art Smith's. It has his vigorous stamp, but the two opening lines still have me gravelled. Am I being obtuse? I don't know whether I like the Auden-ish *coda*. But the two middle verses are grand satire. (AC, 22 Oct. 1941)

Northrop Frye, in the *Canadian Forum*, praised *Contemporary Verse*. "No poem is flat or bad, and all show considerable literary experience," he wrote.

Leo Kennedy's poem was "graceful" though facile, Smith's was "sharply conceived" though "somewhat metallic in sound," Birney's was "arrestingly beautiful," and Floris McLaren's "poignant even if too heavily accented. . . . If you buy this little pamphlet, you will get wit. . . satire. . . music. . . imagination . . . where else can you get all that for two bits?"[12] And a generous, though defensive, welcome came from E.J. Pratt in *Canadian Poetry Magazine*:

> We welcome the appearance of this little sheaf of verse which constitutes Vol. 1, No. 1 of another Canadian quarterly. It is not brought out in competition or conflict with *Canadian Poetry Magazine*, as its main concern is with contemporary techniques while our own magazine. . . has tried to preserve a balance between tradition and modernity. Moreover, we hail any progressive effort which would freshen the quality of our national verse.[13]

The second issue of *Contemporary Verse*—longer but less impressive, less bold than the first—was ready by December. It is a mixed bag, beginning with an effusive poem by Audrey Alexandra Brown and including work by such new contributors as Ralph Gustafson, H.A.V. Green (a friend of Crawley's from Winnipeg), Carol Cassidy, Kay Smith, Ronald Hambleton, and further work from Kennedy, Livesay, McLaren, and Page. Birney remarked in *Canadian Forum*: "The second number of the mimeographed verse-magazine which a group of younger writers has initiated in Vancouver shows an advance in quantity and quality over the promising first issue."[14]

With the third issue of *Contemporary Verse* (March, 1942) Crawley hit his stride. There are still some traditionalists among the contributors, but what gives the issue its particular flavour is the presentation of groups of poems by a single writer (with poems arranged together). The broader representation benefits the poet and gives coherence and depth to the magazine. Years later James Reaney wrote in *Alphabet*, "In looking over *CV* myself I think the reason for its continuing impression, despite the multilith typed production is that the poems are published in groups—Four Poems by so-and-so, Five Poems by etc. so that one gets a chance to see each poem in a field of relatedness, also a fair look at each poet."[15] Miriam Waddington and Raymond Souster made their first appearance in *Contemporary Verse* in this issue and helped to counteract the impression made by A.M. Stephen, Gordon LeClaire, Amelia Wensley, and Helen Geddes—none of whom appeared again in the magazine.

With three issues out and publicity from reviews, modern poets must have known of *Contemporary Verse* by the spring of 1942. Yet Crawley was having a difficult time getting enough good poetry to fill fourteen small pages quarterly. Readers were supporting *Contemporary Verse* but not writers. In April Crawley wrote to Birney:

> Progress with CV has been rather remarkable and if we can add fifty more subscribers and retain a fair percentage of the ones we have through another year we should be able to finance but what really worries me is the paucity of good work that comes through the mill. There has been no dearth of mediocre, traditional writing, church monthly stuff, God about us and feathered birds etc. but far too little exceptional work. Also, I have been struck by the discovery that few of our writers, contrary to the old ideas of poets, send in love poems and none of them sound a note of fortitude and encouragement. (UT, 1942)

Too often Crawley had to use poetry which did not meet his standards in order to get an issue out, and throughout the course of the magazine he was forced to delay issues while he waited for good poetry to arrive. ''Have had three poems from A.M. Stephen,'' he wrote to Floris McLaren while he was working on the third number, ''unremarkable but two of them think I may use'' (FMcL, March 1942). The established poets did not seem to have poetry to submit, or perhaps they were adopting a ''wait and see'' attitude to *Contemporary Verse*. Earle Birney, for example, had written to Crawley in the previous fall: ''Thanks very much for the invitation to submit to your next number. I'll send some things along as soon as I have seen your first issue and get some notion what length and type of verse you might prefer.'' (AC, 6 Oct. 1941).

Still, Crawley was hopeful of finding good material, and he was not limiting his search to established poets. He confided to Birney in April 1942: ''I am on the track of some work from really unknown writers and am hopeful of a find'' (UT). Birney himself seemed more confident of the calibre of *Contemporary Verse* after the third number and submitted two poems for the next issue (''Nocturne'' and ''War Winter''), and three came from James Wreford. The outlook for number four improved, but the future of the magazine was uncertain. ''Floris McLaren came over for a weekend with us,'' Crawley wrote on 28 May to Birney, ''and we discussed the affairs of the quarterly and it seems possible it may be able to keep going and for that we will do our best.'' Crawley thought the March issue of *Contemporary Verse* was ''different'' and ''interesting'' and ''quite up to the standard of many of the verse magazines of other places,'' but he was anxious that it ''should be better and show improvement as the numbers add up'' (UT). A few months later Crawley commented to Birney that ''there is sincerity and straightforward thinking and writing turning up in some places,'' but that ''contemplation is the terribly lacking element'' (UT, nd).

This active correspondence between Earle Birney and Alan Crawley had begun with Crawley's request for poems for *Contemporary Verse*, and it continued throughout the course of the magazine. Crawley and Birney had not known one another at the beginning of the correspondence, but they quickly developed a mutual liking and respect. Crawley encouraged Birney and criticized his work, and Birney provided a friendly ear to listen to the tribulations and triumphs of the magazine. Birney frequently wrote to comment on a specific issue of *Contemporary Verse* or on an individual writer or poem, giving Crawley a valued opinion against which to measure his own standards and choices.

Their comments to each other on the literary scene also bring the period alive in a down-to-earth and intimate way. Birney's letter of 6 October 1941 from Toronto suggests a quickening of interest in poetry in Canada, a new liveliness:

> A.J.M. Smith was here for a few days and I got to know and like him. He has a book of his verse under consideration with a New York publisher: I saw the MS and I think it's going to be one of the best volumes of verse a Canadian has yet issued. He's still a bit too obviously in the Eliot school, but his later work, some of which you may have seen in *20 Cent. Poetry*, etc., has a highly concentrated and half-bawdy kind of humor which is very individual and effective. As you probably know, he is preparing a critical anthology of Can. poetry under a Guggenheim award.

Birney goes on to comment on Pratt's soon-to-be-issued *Dunkirk and Other Verses*:

> The "Dunkirk" itself, if it is all like the passages I have heard Ned read, is perhaps the best thing he's done—despite the popular patness of the theme—and makes Masefield's dutiful performance look sillier than ever. Ned's gusto, which the Brébeuf theme scared out of him, is back, and he manages even to find occasion for a few private jokes concerning some Toronto personalities, who turn up in Channel rowboats, with slightly altered names.

"A special cheap issue of the Dunkirk alone," Birney added, "is being rushed for the Christmas trade, and, with Simpson's buying 2000 copies in advance, it looks as if at last a Canadian poet may make some money without losing his soul" (AC).

In April 1942, Crawley sent Birney some round-about praise from L.A. MacKay who had given a talk on Canadian poetry for a university extension course. "After the talk someone pinned him down with question of whose writing he thought the best in Canada today," Crawley wrote, "and I understand he said that your work was the most remarkable." (UT). In May a hurried letter came back from Birney with the news that "At any moment I expect to enter the army. I'm trying frantically to wind up my civilian affairs," Birney wrote: "I will have to delay the pleasure of meeting you until the war is over. If I ever get the time to write anything before that happy date (which is unlikely) I shall keep in touch with you'' (AC, 21 May 1942).

Contemporary Verse 4 came out in mid-summer 1942, more substantial and finished, with its ''Editor's Note'' at the beginning and ''Notes on Contributors'' at the end. There are fewer and larger groups of poems: three each by James Wreford and Anne Marriott, four by Nathan Ralph, and two by Earle Birney—satisfying chunks to chew and digest. Variety is the keynote, both in subject matter and technique. Wreford's left-wing statements are balanced by Ralph's undidactic descriptive poems; Birney's vigorous alliterative rhythms in ''War Winter,'' by Marriott's deliberately prosaic and mundane tone in ''Rest Room.'' Social themes dominate the issue as they do throughout the war years. ''I consider number four the best by far of all the issues,'' Crawley wrote to the founding committee, ''and so hope to think of each succeeding number. There's a goal my lad to strive for'' (FMcL, Oct. 1942).

With *Contemporary Verse* less than a year old, Alan Crawley was already embarked on the mammoth correspondence that became as important to poets in the forties as the magazine itself. Instead of rejection slips—''I thought that with this new magazine having no established standard or reputation a formal letter such as used by most editors seemed too formal and a bit swanky'' (FMcL, nd)—Crawley decided to comment on manuscripts he returned, giving his reasons for rejecting the poem or making suggestions for revision. It turned out to be an enormous amount of work for Crawley, since he received about five hundred manuscripts a year, but a valuable service to poets who came to rely on Crawley's astute, impartial judgement. If the poet showed promise, Crawley offered to read and criticize his work on a more intensive level. P.K. Page was an early find and when Crawley offered to comment on her work, Page wrote back, ''I am 'post-hasting' an answer off to you to say *by all means*. . . . At the moment I am on my own in Montreal knowing practically no one who writes and having no critical eyes scan what I am writing and should welcome anything you have to say.'' (AC, 1 Dec. 1941). Later, in May 1942, she wrote:

> How grand of you to write to me about the poems. You've no idea what a stimulating thing it has been—this contact with you, even across so many miles. It is doubly good to get praises from someone who is unafraid to damn. And your letter yesterday arrived with two others which told me I was ruining my chances by publishing such stuff and they hoped I would not continue in that vein. All of which gives one cause to think.

By then Page was a member of the newly formed *Preview* group, and she added in the letter: ''I'd love to know your ideas on the Preview crowd. It is a strange group to be associated with—especially as I am the only non-political member'' (AC). Even though she was a *Preview* writer, Page continued to rely on Crawley for criticism and support. In 1945, for example, she wrote about "Round Trip":

> I have made a number of changes in the poem—working from your letter and at this point the whole thing seems to be on such an incredibly pedestrian level that I can hardly bear it. That is one of my major problems—rewriting. None of my work can stand such scrutiny. While I polish the carvings on the archways the archways crumble! (AC, 25 March 1945)

In 1946, Page sent a copy of her first collection of poems—*As Ten As Twenty*—to Alan and Jean Crawley, and wrote: "Whether you like it or not, I feel this is partly your book. Alan's criticism, help and encouragement since CV's beginning have contributed more than any other thing to what progress I may have made in the last few years" (AC, 4 Nov. 1946).

Seasoned poets benefited from Crawley's criticism too. Dorothy Livesay's poetic output was down to a trickle when she started visiting Alan Crawley. "Soon I began to write again, I think under his influence; then I began showing him the poems, getting his criticism of them. He helped me a bit—he tried to make my language more what he called 'modern.' "[16] And Earle Birney often discussed poems with Crawley and relied on his suggestions for revision. "Man on a Tractor" refused to take shape, and Birney wrote to Crawley: "I won't object to any cutting you want to do in making use of that piece—I should in fact be grateful if someone would do a good pruning job on it for me!" (AC, 15 Oct. 1945). The poem was awkward, mainly because of jarring shifts from colloquial to more formal language, and Crawley concentrated on diction and transitions. Birney wrote back after seeing the changes: "I was trying to slide back into his language. . . for variety and directness. Perhaps this time it rings awkwardly. I don't think I changed it in the proof, but if you feel it better the other way, i.e. indirect speech, go ahead" (AC, nd).

As Alan Crawley rounded out his first year of editing *Contemporary Verse*, the literary climate of Canada was changing. *Preview*, the coterie magazine from Montreal, had begun in March and its rival *First Statement* would appear in the late fall. *Preview* may have been one of the reasons why there was not more poetry coming across Crawley's desk in the spring and summer of 1942. The magazine appeared monthly and devoted roughly half of its space to poetry (it worked out to about six poems per issue in the first year). Certainly *Preview* had snared P.K. Page, who during its period of publication disappeared almost entirely from *Contemporary Verse*. The Montreal magazine could not have been more unlike *Contemporary Verse*. It was partisan, militant, esoteric, and self-conscious.

"This is no magazine," the much-quoted "Statement" in *Preview* 1 reads, "it presents five Montreal writers who recently formed themselves into a group for the purposes of mutual discussion and criticism and who hope, through these selections, to try out their work before a somewhat larger public." The *Preview* writers proposed to write from a common political stance: "All anti-fascists, we feel that the existence of a war between democratic culture and the paralyzing forces of dictatorship only intensifies the writer's obligation to work. Now, more than ever, creative and experimental writing must be kept alive and there must be no retreat from the intellectual frontier." They advocated a particular literary approach: "the poets amongst us look forward, perhaps optimistically, to a possible fusion between the lyric and didactic elements in modern verse, a combination of vivid, arresting imagery, and the capacity to 'sting' with social content and criticism." [17] The poetry in *Preview* had a strong left-wing political flavour; it was apparent that Auden, Spender, and Dylan Thomas had arrived in Canada.

Obviously in reply to *Preview*'s political, coterie stance, Crawley hurried to clarify the policy of *Contemporary Verse* in the June 1942 issue. "A glance at the note on contributors at the back of this number shows that CONTEMPORARY VERSE is not the chapbook of a limited or local group of writers," Crawley wrote, and he declared that "the contents of each number will at once dispel any charge that it exists to press political propaganda, particular social readjustment or literary trend" (4:3). "Chapbook of a limited or local group of writers," "press political propaganda"; these are, for Crawley, argumentative and militant statements. Crawley believed that the work of a poetry magazine was to publish poetry, and he had no particular literary approach to eschew and no axes to grind. He wanted to encourage and publish poetry that was alive and fresh and relevant; poetry that was sensitive and honest and of the best possible quality. He hoisted his own liberal banner:

> The aims of CONTEMPORARY VERSE are simple and direct and seem worthy and worthwhile. These aims are to entice and stimulate the writing and reading of poetry and to provide means for its publication free from restraint of politics, prejudices and placations, and to keep open its pages to poetry that is sincere in theme and treatment and technique. (4:3)

The first four numbers of *Contemporary Verse* reflect Crawley's eclectic editorial policy. There are fifty-five poems as various in treatment as in theme, from established and unknown poets, from across Canada and parts of the United States. Crawley was not yet satisfied with the standard of poetry that he published, but he was confident that he had chosen the best available, and he hoped the quality would improve now that poets had a place to try out their work. He and the founding committee decided to continue *Contemporary Verse* for another year:

> More than three hundred and fifty manuscripts have been read and in many of these there is a richness of thought, diction and imagination that strengthens my conviction that a considerable national contribution to creative art in Canada may be made in the continuance of publication of a quarterly of CONTEMPORARY VERSE. (4:4)

Hardly had Alan Crawley made his decision to continue *Contemporary Verse* when a third little magazine appeared in Canada.

First Statement was produced by John Sutherland, Betty Sutherland, Robert Simpson, Keith MacLellan, and Audrey Aikman, and it was, ambitiously, to appear every two weeks. "We are going on a diet of cheap, mimeographed paper, a kind of literary bread and water. We intend asking no charge for the magazine, to prevent the petty hope of making a profit. We are going to rid ourselves of practical encumbrances, to have freedom in which to move."[18] By the third issue Sutherland had become more practical. He announced that there would be a fee charged for the magazine (one dollar per year) and that contributions would be paid for at the rate of half a cent a word, and he defined the policy of the magazine. "We believe that the business of a Canadian magazine, in a country where the literature receives a minimum of publicity, is to serve Canadian writers only, and to direct its attention primarily to the Canadian public." *First Statement* would, therefore, try to print "the various modes and types of writing as they are found in Canada"; and Sutherland hoped the magazine would "become the mirror of this variety" and in so doing "provide the Canadian reader with the freedom of choice that he requires."[19]

First Statement did print a variety of writing—but the authors came almost exclusively from the east, and because of this geographical bias the picture it mirrored was distorted, or at least limited. Little poetry was published in the first few months of *First Statement* (about three poems per issue), and it was unimposing except for the work of *Preview* writers Patrick Anderson and P.K. Page and of Audrey Aikman and Kay Smith. After combining with *Western Free Lance*—a Vancouver magazine that had published its first, and only, issue in September 1942—Sutherland thought that *First Statement* would be a truly representative national magazine, but there was no apparent change. Earle Birney, for example, never appeared in *First Statement* (or in *Preview*), nor did Dorothy Livesay, who commented, long afterwards in 1969, on the eastern bias of *First Statement*:

> In Canada we've been rifled by cliques, and we still are you know. Every city has its circle and its fans and its. . . self-adulation going on, but Alan was completely free of this. And he did get people from all parts of the country writing. . . . I mean the Montreal group around *First Statement* was a fascinating group, but it was a clique.[20]

Alan Crawley was both pleased and worried about this proliferation of little magazines. They were evidence of interest and activity in poetry writing, but there was little good poetry being written in the fall and winter of 1942. He wrote to Birney:

> I am greatly encouraged at the very evident interest in Canada in what is being done in the arts. . . the two latest Preview and First Statement are so well worth while and seem to have a character of their own and a vigour that is growing in spite of what they have to contend with. Whether there is room and support for them and for CV remains to be seen.

''We suffer from some handicaps that they appear to have not met with yet,'' Crawley enlarged, ''The isolation of this western coast is hard to overcome, there are too few young people here who are willing to lend a hand and I am so disabled that what I can do seems sometimes so pitifully little to what I would do and wish to accomplish'' (UT, nd). The ''isolation'' of the west coast was a problem; even if Crawley had lived in Vancouver (Caulfeild seemed quite distant from Vancouver in the early forties), it would have been easier for him to get to poets—to talk to them, to suggest changes in poems, clarify obscure lines, encourage more writing, relay news and comments from other poets; in sum to create that climate that stimulates writing.

Added to the limited amount of good poetry available for publication and to Crawley's isolation, there was the additional problem of the prevailing antipathy to modern poetry in Canada. As such poetry was naturalized and became more relevant to Canada, support grew, yet readers were justified in their impatience with the awkward imitations of British and American poetry that still dominated ''modern'' Canadian poetry in the early forties. Not only was early forties' poetry derivative, it was also pessimistic. Lionel Stevenson, a traditionalist but not unsympathetic to new approaches in poetry, was discouraged by the first few issues of *Contemporary Verse*. He had supported this new poetry magazine, but he seemed visibly upset by the ''mood of whining and self-pity and frustration which has dominated the 'modern poetry' of the present generation'' and which he found too much in evidence in the magazine: ''I can therefore not summon up much enthusiasm for a selection that continues to harp so monotonously on this single string.'' Stevenson found the poetry in *Contemporary Verse* 1 derivative and depressing. ''The techniques of the new school, with its mutings and discords and 'dead string' noises, are effectively employed by your contributors, and form a further barrier between their poetry and the service of the ordinary people'' (FMcL, 29 Nov. 1941). Looking back in a recent letter on his reaction to *Contemporary Verse* 1, Stevenson enlarged on why he felt so disappointed:

> I hoped that a new venture in Canadian poetry, such as this one, would show a fresh and native talent that was not dominated by alien models as earlier Canadian poets had been in their day. Instead, I found the fashionable tones and moods of Eliot-Auden, which I was beginning to find tedious in English and American periodicals. (JMcC, 3 Aug. 1970)

But, he added, "As the subsequent issues came out, I soon changed my opinion as to the magazine's merits, and with the advantage of hindsight I realize that the first number marked the debut of a periodical that was of outstanding significance in modern Canadian poetry."

Resistance to the kind of poetry being written by the majority of modern Canadian poets in the early years of the forties did not come only from traditionalists. W.W.E. Ross, perhaps the most accomplished though least known of the modern poets of the period, read *Contemporary Verse* for a year, then wrote to Floris McLaren to cancel his subscription:

> To speak frankly, I have seen very little of interest in the magazine since Earle Birney's "Hands" and a few other pieces in the first two or three issues. It may seem all right to keep on republishing Auden, but why try to repeat Eliot as well? Isn't the time for that passing? Anyway, this perpetual whining about the terrible state of things has lost its freshness. One might say it did some time since. Satire, with some bite to it, and specific objects of attack, might be of more interest—as positive, rather than negative,—than these fragments from the slightly crumbling Eliot-Auden wailing-wall. (FMcL, 7 June 1943)

Probably Ross's own progress toward an individualistic, natural idiom made him even less tolerant of the general derivativeness of Canadian poetry at this time.

But generally things were brighter for Alan Crawley and for modern poetry in the fall of 1942 when *Contemporary Verse* celebrated its first precarious year of publication. The magazine was known and was establishing itself as an eclectic magazine of real quality. With *Preview* and *First Statement* stirring up interest in the east and three publication outlets available, modern poets were assured of being heard, if they had anything to say. Klein's *Hath Not a Jew,* Birney's *David and Other Poems*, and Gustafson's *Anthology of Canadian Poetry* were now available and were being read. Canadian poetry was finally swinging around to modernism. In the next few years modern Canadian poetry lost its blatant derivativeness, overcame much of its gaucherie and rawness, and, most important, found a native, natural, effective idiom. Alan Crawley and *Contemporary Verse* played a significant part in this naturalizing process, and the changes in Canadian poetry were graphically shown in the magazine.

CHAPTER TWO

Modernism Naturalized: *Contemporary Verse* 1941-1946

The forties' movement in Canada had two phases. The first, which John Sutherland anthologized in *Other Canadians. . . 1940-1946*, established modernism in Canada; the second, more amorphous, saw poets exploring their worlds as the centrifugal force of the war passed away and the need to create an indigenous literature was fulfilled. *Contemporary Verse* reflects these phases. Numbers one to twenty show a marked concern about the war and about the situation of poetry in Canada. Each new book of poetry is greeted by the magazine's reviewers with the enthusiasm pioneers give new arrivals, but also with wariness. The poetry published in the successive issues gains enormously in poise, flexibility, and assurance. Numbers twenty to thirty-nine have greater variety—both in theme and in technique—the verse is of better quality; one senses the victory of new finds. But uneasiness is also evident in some poets, and in others a heaviness as they try to abandon public utterance in favour of more private speech. A few are excessively obscure.

Technically, in rhythm, imagery, and verse forms, forties' poetry is notably varied; but a lyric approach, an overriding social concern, and the focus of the war gives it a distinct and recognizable flavour. In the 1948 edition of the *Book of Canadian Poetry* A.J.M. Smith wrote:

> The poetry of the forties grows out of a sense of being involved in the whole complex life of our time—its politics, its society, its economics—and of being involved in it in a deeply personal way that touches the sensibilities, the mind, and the physical being of the poet. This is perhaps the common attitude which unites all the very different individual poets into a single recognizable school.[1]

This development towards a natural, idiomatic poetry is clearly reflected in *Contemporary Verse*. It is a measure of Alan Crawley's eclecticism that the magazine captures all of the moods and trends of Canadian poetry in this period. In this book, however, only the major poets and the general movement of poetry during the period will be discussed.

Alan Crawley's efforts to prevent *Contemporary Verse* from being a "chapbook of a limited or local group of writers" (4:3) were successful; every modern poet in Canada with the exception of W.W.E. Ross and Patrick Anderson published in *Contemporary Verse*. Nevertheless, certain dominant figures emerged. In the 1941-1946 period Dorothy Livesay, Earle Birney, Miriam Waddington, P.K. Page, Floris McLaren, and James Wreford contributed the largest number of poems, supported by substantial contributions from L.A. MacKay, Anne Marriott, Louis Dudek, Raymond Souster, and Kay Smith.

Earle Birney's war poems were the best of this genre to appear in *Contemporary Verse* (and in Canada). Poems such as "Hands," "War Winter," "Nocturne," "Letter Home," "Within These Concerned Days," and "Time Bomb" have authenticity, immediacy, and universality. Birney never adopted a patriotic stance; he wrote as a humanitarian anguished at the suffering man was inflicting upon man, even more anguished at the knowledge that something in man himself had caused this incredible holocaust: "Within the statesman's ribs,/Within my own, the timebombstick" (15:7).

There is also a pervading sense of the war in Dorothy Livesay's poems, though few of them overtly discuss it. Like Birney, Livesay saw the order of nature as normal and advised man to re-establish communication with the natural world. Raymond Souster, in "Home Front," Floris McLaren, in "Dark Departure," A.M. Klein, in "Not All the Perfumes of Arabia," and James McDermott, in "As Regards Detonating," all treat the themes of war, man's destructiveness, and his alienation from nature.

Other poets examine the depersonalized lives of people in a newly urbanized and industrialized Canada. Anne Marriott attempts to capture the sense of boredom and meaninglessness in "Rest Room," where there is no rest for the "taut clock-watcher":

> Seeking the clock-face, seeking the stairs, elevator,
> Scrambling back to the clock-face, staring
> To see only a minute has passed while you strained an hour. (4:10)

The people who gather on Nathan Ralph's "Six O'Clock Car" and "fold a journal about a bearded face" are not seen as real people but as impersonal, impermanent colours:

And colors on the car
        of green and mauve, black and brown
leave off quietly . . . empty . . .
the car goes on. (4:13)

In ''Sorrow,'' Miriam Waddington exposes the government's callous treatment of the ignorant, poor, and ill. ''Sorrow is not a kind sister/Trailing dispensation in her wide sleeves,'' it is ''the strict almshouse where comfort is doled by government regulation''; and ''Only the pious adepts, practiced at talking poormouth/Are granted the foursquare peace'' (5:12). People who are ''different'' are punished too; Jews, in ''The Bond,'' and immigrants in ''Immigrant, Second Generation.''

P.K. Page is more psychological in her approach to the isolation of the individual. Her people are often ''permanent tourists'' in life, onlookers not participants; locked within themselves and behind masks. The journey motif is used in two of Page's war period poems in *Contemporary Verse*, ''The Traveller'' in the December 1942 issue and ''Round Trip'' in April 1945. Cullen, in ''The Traveller,'' never finds a meaningful relationship with another person, nor a meaning to life:

he volunteered at once and went to war
wondering what on earth he was fighting for.
He knew there was a reason but couldn't find it
and walked to battle half an inch behind it. (6:9)

The tone of ''Round Trip'' is more introspective and malignant. The white, neat, flat, incredibly well-prepared traveller boards the train, leaving behind:

the tightly frozen rivers of his blood
the plateaux of his boredom
and the bare
buttonholes that his pallid eyes had cut. (13:3)

But his fantastic journey is circular. He ends back at the start where ''everything's the same;/Forever, everywhere for him, the same'' (13:7).

Dorothy Livesay's early forties' poetry demonstrates the shift in sensibility as a flexible, self-assured modernism became the norm in Canada. Livesay's handling of her material is surer, more fluid and natural in *Contemporary Verse* 5 than in her three-poem sequence in the second number of the magazine. The earlier poems (probably written in the late thirties) are not satisfying wholes; they are didactic and strident and see the disorder in society as something external to the individual—arising out of an inequitable economic or political system, not out of anything within man. Implicit in these poems is the message that the world can be improved by finding a better system; or, alternately, that the individual can escape into an inner world. In the later sequence, the poet has matured. She is squarely in and of the world and knows that it is people, not systems, that must change. She looks to nature for comfort and (perhaps) salvation:

> Be earthward bound; and here
> In the strata of flown flowers
> And skeleton of leaf, set self down
> Hurry ear to ground. (5:8)

But the poems are not optimistic; Livesay fears "We are late sleepers, drugged in dark/Aliens all, to morning" (5:7).

In his review of *Day and Night* in the April 1944 issue of *Contemporary Verse*, L.A. MacKay divides Livesay's work into two phases—the late formative and the early mature—with the war as the turning point. In the late formative period, MacKay finds in Livesay's work "a contortion of phrase which seems to be the result of an intellectual struggle to express completely something that is not completely and directly apprehended." Her mature work is "poetry of one understood and mentally assimilated world, rather than two disconnected worlds, one rejected and one hoped for" (10:15). MacKay's division can be explored further. Livesay's early "contortion of phrase" may have its roots in her "struggle to express completely something that is not completely and directly apprehended"; but more likely it results from her struggle to objectify her experience into a poem that can be directly apprehended by the reader—a skill which she and many of her contemporaries had not mastered before the war.

Younger poets who began writing poetry during the early forties were not troubled by the nineteenth-century–modern conflict as the poets of the twenties and thirties were; they were troubled by the lack of an indigenous modern literature to grow up on. P.K. Page's early poetry shows her working to assimilate foreign influences into a Canadian consciousness and voice, and she is typical of the many Canadian poets who had to learn to be Canadian in their poetry. Her sources in "Ecce Homo" and in "The Crow" are obvious, and her idiom is foreign. "Blackout" in the second *Contemporary Verse* is strongly influenced by Auden, but the vocabulary is less intellectual, and a conversational tone is more nearly approximated. A year later, in December 1942, Page has moved away from imitation in her breezy, ironic, narrative poem "The Traveller" (6:7). The poem does not have the characteristic Page imprint yet, and there is still awkward phrasing and un-Canadian diction ("factory-made goods," "dreadful town," "lodgings"), but it is not patently derivative. By the end of the war Page had evolved a distinctive poetic voice arising naturally out of Canadian experiences, as her poem "Morning, Noon and Night" shows:

> Dropped from some great height they flop at noon,
> liquid and lazy with the heat, upon
> the bright green grass beneath the trees, between
> the grey of public stone;
> and hardly know their wish
> and hardly guess
> themselves as more than surface indolence. (19:3)

Louis Dudek was at home with the Canadian idiom even in his earliest poems, but he had difficulty moulding the language into effective poetry. In "Night Scene" in the March 1943 issue of *Contemporary Verse*, he is too prosaic:

> Somewhere I hear the notes of a piano
> And into my head drift the words of a poem
> Which a while ago I was reading. (7:11)

and in "Morning," from the same issue, he lapses into affectation:

> Sun-dance on a banister,
> Pea-shooter sun on roof,
> Pop-corns exploding at street corners
> Sun-sliding, sun, dazzle-proof. (7:11)

Two years later in "Midsummer, Adirondacks" (14:11) Dudek still shows the influence of Dylan Thomas, but by 1947, when nine of his poems appeared in the winter issue of *Contemporary Verse*, Dudek's language is both natural and effective.

Such *Contemporary Verse* poets as Anne Marriott and Floris McLaren remained transition poets even though they explored modern themes. In 1943, in the first edition of the *Book of Canadian Poetry*, A.J.M. Smith divided modern poetry into two categories—"Modern Native" and "Modern Cosmopolitan." The division he made is actually between transition poetry and modern poetry. The poets listed under the "Native Tradition" have not yet acquired a modern sensibility—their work still shows the struggle between the romantic tradition and the attitudes and techniques of modernism—while those grouped under the "Cosmopolitan Tradition" have achieved a modern voice. What irritated John Sutherland was the derivativeness of this cosmopolitan modernism. During the war modernism was naturalized, and an indigenous modern poetry evolved that was Canadian "in the only way that is worth anything, implicitly and inevitably" (these are Smith's words from the 1948 edition of the *Book of Canadian Poetry*).[2] This was the real accomplishment of the early forties' poets; and in his continuing work of sifting through the manuscripts that came across his desk, criticizing and sending poems back for revision, selecting and publishing the largest body of poetry during the forties, and reviewing most of the books of poetry published during the decade, Alan Crawley was intimately a part of this accomplishment. Crawley's ideas about poetry and the standards he set for *Contemporary Verse* were, therefore, significant shaping forces on early forties' poetry.

Alan Crawley was not a theorizer about poetry. He responded intuitively and personally to a poem, and he had the "taste" to know if a poem was good or bad regardless of its terms of reference. Crawley liked a poem that said something and "said" well. He responded to energy and rhythm and sound. He was chary and parsimonious in adding to the small store of poems that met his exacting standards of excellence, and he was quick and frank in his criticism of mediocrity and insincerity. "Every book of poetry on my shelves must pay space rent in at least two poems to read again and again," Crawley wrote in a review of *David and Other Poems* (6:15).

Sound in poetry was of crucial importance to Alan Crawley. He approached poetry as an auditor, listening to each new poem several times over. Later he used a tape recorder, but in the forties someone—usually his wife Jean—read him the poem several times over until he had memorized it or typed it in braille for him to "say" to himself until he had fully apprehended its sound and rhythmic pattern. With this as a basis he moved into a full appreciation of the poem, incorporating the thought, imagery, and verse form into the sound pattern. His approach was first sensuous, then intellectual. A letter to Earle Birney in early February 1943 illustrates Crawley's concern with sound in a poem:

> On the following Tuesday night I heard the Story Teller read your David and liked his reading of it. . .but inconsequent as it may seem, again as before when I had heard it read by Jean to me, the lines that struck and annoyed me are those. . ."on my ripped boots of his blood". . . such a cavil but when I am so dependent on my ear for all the poetry I get a harsh unpleasant line does irritate. (UT, nd)[3]

Reviewing *Now is Time* in 1946, Crawley again discussed the sound in Birney's poems. "There is a new power in Mr. Birney's writing. The late poems show this in the smoothness of line from which grit of hard unusual words have been cast out and in the strong noun unpropped by adjective" (17:18).

"Reading the poems obviously written within the last twenty years I am struck by their vitality and strength," Crawley wrote referring to the poetry in Gustafson's *Anthology of Canadian Poetry* (5:16). Of Patrick Anderson's *A Tent for April* he said: "The impression that has pleased and persisted most strongly with me is that of extreme vitality and energy, springing and fed from Mr. Anderson's feeling for movement, so skillfully and sensitively translated into words" (13:16). Energy, intensity, and vitality were the essential components of a poem for Crawley, all the better if coupled with vivid fresh imagery. He liked P.K. Page's imagery and Dudek's and Reaney's. "What is perhaps the most distinctive element" in Page's poetry in *As Ten As Twenty* (which Crawley judged to be "a remarkable first book") "is her wealth of imagery drawn from wide and varied sources, sharp and startling with the force of the personality they reveal" (19:18). Of Dudek, Crawley wrote, "Over and over again we find this poet taking the raw materials of poetry and from them building a logical and often magical sequence of connected images, sensations, and suggestions in organized association and musical arrangement"; and of Reaney, "His poetry is sometimes derivative but it is never conventional and always is charged with his individual rather macabre imagination and is lovely in the unusual brilliant clusters of sounds and images" (23:21-22).

Alan Crawley liked to feel the poet was writing out of his own intensely felt experiences and had something significant to say. A poem was not for moralizing or for grinding axes, but it was for communication. "No poetry can be written unless the writer has absorbed something from the world about him and from the effects of this is able to say his reactions and feelings caused by this absorption and reflection in some different and lovely way" (FMcL, 1 Feb. 1937), Crawley wrote to Floris McLaren advising her on the selection of poems for *Frozen Fire*. He reiterated this belief ten years later, singling out a quotation from the writings of A.C. Bradley that is "so good a caption for this magazine or to be a framed motto on its official wall that I shall repeat it":

> If a poem is to be anything like great it must, in one sense, be concerned with the present. Whatever its subject may be, it must express something living in the mind from which it comes and the minds to which it goes. Wherever its body is, its soul must be here and now. (23:18)

Crawley (like many of his contemporaries) seemed immune to the strong didactic quality of the poetry of the first half of the forties. In 1942, while reviewing *David and Other Poems*, he noted: "Mr. Birney has no social problem to pose and no ethical code to expound. He is not absorbed in exploring wide and deep ideas. His writing is free of didacticism. . ." (6:14). In 1945 he described Patrick Anderson's poems in *A Tent for April*: "The poems are unangered and unresentful, and glory be to heaven, they have no whine of persecution nor whimper of self-pity, and there is remarkable absence of propaganda, prediction and prescription for these or future times '' (13:16). Later on, with the distancing of time and with new trends in poetry, Crawley became more sensitive to didacticism. In ten years ''Earle Birney has changed his technique very little apart from progressive refining and developing, and a regrettable almost complete elimination of expression of passion or of deep emotion,'' Crawley commented, reviewing *Trial of a City and Other Verse*. ''The axe is still taken to grinding although it is now more cunningly concealed'' (39:24-25).

There was no specific genre, theme, or technique that Alan Crawley preferred or favoured in *Contemporary Verse*. There were, however, two kinds of poetry uncongenial to him—imagist and narrative poetry—although examples of both genres can be found in the magazine. The absence of ''meaning'' and of personal involvement in imagist poems could explain why Crawley did not particularly like them, although the strong visual component in imagist poems and their rhythmical plainness might also be factors. ''I never cared for W.W.E. Ross's poems,'' Crawley remarked in an interview, ''they did not say much to me.'' In his review of Raymond Knister's *Collected Poems* he disagreed with ''the Smith-Livesay-Kennedy tributes and estimations'' of Knister's strongly imagistic work. ''Take out of the section *Men and Animals* the dreary genealogical cataloguing of *Row of Stalls*, and the unsuccessful *Poisons*, add to the poems left *After Exile*—and you have the poetry by which Raymond Knister may be remembered'' (31:22).

''I do not as you know like narrative verse, unless of very exceptional power and beauty,'' Crawley reminded Floris McLaren after he had advised her to drop ''Gene's Bride'' from her *Frozen Fire* collection (FMcL, 1 Feb. 1937). When Crawley admitted this bias to Earle Birney five years later—''The poem [David] is a fine bit and in spite of my dislike of narrative poetry you have done a good thing in it and I am glad it has got so much praise from reviewers and readers'' (UT, nd)—Birney rapped his editorial knuckles sharply:

> Am amazed that you should admit to a ''dislike'' of narrative poetry. If that is really so, you are ruled out from enjoying most of the great poetic literature—Homer, the *Aeneid*, Chaucer, Dante, most of Milton, Goethe, Byron, Shelley, Keats, and a good deal of Wordsworth. The form has admittedly been unfashionable of late, but what have we to do with fashions? Leave them to the IODE and CAA. The most promising poetry editor in Canada should be above prejudices which relate to a whole *form*. It is like a great horticulturist saying that he won't grow peaches because he doesn't like their fuzz, or that he is only interested in apples under 5 ounces. (AC,20 Feb. 1943)

In spite of these biases (which had scanty effect since little imagist or narrative poetry was being written), Alan Crawley was the most eclectic poetry editor in

Canada during the forties. By the end of 1946 when *Contemporary Verse* was at its mid point, he had published almost three hundred poems by seventy poets—the largest, most impressive, and most representative collection of early forties' work in Canada. In the same period *First Statement* (and later *Northern Review*) published about one hundred and fifty poems, the work of some thirty-five poets; and *Preview* substantially fewer, perhaps one hundred poems, almost exclusively the work of the *Preview* group.[4] Louis Dudek, Irving Layton, and Raymond Souster were the major contributors to *First Statement* after 1943, with Miriam Waddington, Kay Smith, Audrey Aikman, and some members of the *Preview* group also having work published in the magazine.

By far the greater part of *Contemporary Verse*'s pages is given over to poetry, but beginning with the fifth issue in September 1942, Crawley included a review section that discussed all of the important books of poetry that were published during the life of the magazine. Next to the annual "Letters in Canada" in the *University of Toronto Quarterly*, the *Contemporary Verse* reviews constitute the most comprehensive assessment of forties' poetry to come out of the period. Crawley did most of the reviewing, Dorothy Livesay did some, and occasionally L.A. MacKay and Floris McLaren helped out. Crawley's reviews are brief, impressionistic, and free from literary and academic jargon. Lister Sinclair referred to them as "tiny critical notes. . .worth their weight in gold" on *Critically Speaking* in 1950. Crawley's aim in reviewing was to highlight the main characteristics and provide a general assessment of the poetry and to entice the reader into his own exploration of the book. He was impatient with the close textual analysis pioneered by the "new criticism," and he did not use book reviews to express his own ideas and theories about poetry and poets. "I have seen NR and the review of Counterpoint, much of which I like and agree with," Crawley wrote to Anne Wilkinson, "but why all this bother and pretence of great foresight, insight, and the unimportant trimmings which are considered necessary for every book review?" (UT, 8 Nov. 1951). From the mid-forties on, Crawley was a regular reviewer on the Canadian Broadcasting Corporation programme *Critically Speaking*. In his broadcasts he combined his brief criticisms with a reading of a selection of the poet's work. After he did a programme on A.M. Klein in 1947, Klein wrote to thank him, saying "It was most gratifying for me to know that the poems which you were reading were being heard across Canada," and adding:

> I think too that you are to be congratulated upon the very impressive delivery which you gave to these verses, and I particularly was touched by the poems that you chose. Concluding your reading with "Jerusalem Next Year, Next Year Jerusalem" was to my mind a particularly effective gesture. (AC, 16 May 1947)

Livesay's reviews are not impartial like Crawley's. She liked causes and she liked a fight. In the June 1943 issue of *Contemporary Verse*, for example, she lumps four chapbooks together—M. Eugenie Perry, *Hearing a Far Call*; Mary Elizabeth Colman, *For This Freedom Too*; Evelyn Eaton, *Birds Before Dawn*; and Anne Marriott, *Salt Marsh*—and dismissed them in one paragraph: "Ten years ago we spat at sentimental lyricism, bedecked with nature's more obvious outer garments; and we cried out for ideas, and a genuine interpretation of the Canadian people in poetry. The result, if judged by these four booklets, is disastrous" (8:13).

These were exciting and productive but not easy years for Alan Crawley and *Contemporary Verse*. The magazine had its ups and downs. There was seldom enough poetry that met Crawley's standards to fill sixteen pages quarterly (occasionally in these years *Contemporary Verse* was eighteen or twenty pages). Crawley wrote to poets for manuscripts, reminded, encouraged, and cajoled; and then he often had to send submissions back for revision. Subscriptions and finances never reached a comfortable state and wartime restrictions on paper and printing caused frustrating and embarrassing delays in publication. "The quarterly has had more than its share of trouble this summer, running into snags in paper shortage and Government priorities and restrictions and so there has been a terrific delay in getting out the June issue," Crawley wrote to A.J.M. Smith on 22 October 1943 (UT). Sometimes it seemed impossible to Crawley that even the combined efforts of himself, Floris McLaren, and the publishing committee could keep the magazine going. He worried about it to Earle Birney who wrote back: "I do hope Contemporary Verse can continue. It deserves to, more than any other publication of its kind in Canada right now" (AC, 20 Feb. 1943). "Once again CONTEMPORARY VERSE is long overdue," Crawley wrote to the readers in the July 1944 issue. "The causes for delay are so common to most magazines that excuses would be tiresome and explanations are, I hope, unnecessary" (11:2). There was another long delay after this issue (the October number had to be omitted), and Crawley apologized in January. "The staff hope to overcome publishing difficulties and return to the scheduled four issues in 1945" (12:2). Subscribers were frequently reminded to pay up, for "every reader and every dollar is precious," and letters similar to this one of April 1945 were sent out to drum up subscriptions:

> CONTEMPORARY VERSE fills a particular niche in Canadian poetry. The editor is ready to continue with the work of selecting and preparing, the committee is willing to aid him in every way possible; but the urgent necessity is to have on hand the modest finances requisite for production. (AC)

The eastern little magazines were not faring any better. By late 1943 *Preview* was inviting contributions of both manuscripts and money. Earlier in the year *First Statement* had started a similar fund to expand and print the magazine and had reduced the frequency of publication from every two weeks, to monthly, then bi-monthly. Crawley discussed the two magazines with Earle Birney in the summer of 1945:

> Preview went through a shaking up in the last few months with Patrick Anderson forsaking it to take over En Masse mainly political and Pat Page now in Victoria. I gather that Page did most of the stenographic work in the past and was one of the chief stays in management. There was a rumour that Preview was to combine with First Statement but the last issue of the former shows a new lease of life with Klein and Neufville Shaw editing. First Statement is now coming out every two months and is doing some good work. (UT, 12 June 1945)

In the winter of 1945 *Preview* and *First Statement* did merge into *Northern Review* with John Sutherland as editor. It was less of a merger, really, than a closing down of *Preview* and the end of a distinct phase in the development of Canadian poetry. The work of *Preview* was finished. It had been a place where a small group of writers tried out new work of a particular style and political orientation. With the end of the war, the establishment of other publishing outlets, new poetic interests, and the dispersal of the group, the need for the special coterie support of *Preview* disappeared. A.M. Klein kept the magazine going for a time but was doubtless grateful for its graceful exit into *Northern Review*. With the withdrawal of the *Preview* writers after Sutherland's highly critical review of Robert Finch's *Poems* (in the sixth number), *Northern Review* seemed, more than ever, *First Statement* newly named. Raymond Souster has suggested that the animosity between *Preview* and *First Statement* was the basis of the creativity of this period:

> While the two magazines still continued, (in late 1944) hostilities were over. And soon it was open to question just how much of an integral part of this literary movement had nourished itself on what was essentially a meaningless feud, because the last issue of "Preview" appeared not long after, and I could almost read then the first signs of disintegration.[5]

Northern Review, which appeared irregularly, was well printed and broadly oriented to the arts, and it carried some interesting critical discussions (especially those of Sutherland).[6] The poetry was of mixed quality and small in volume—about twenty pages of poetry per year. Alan Crawley wrote to Earle Birney that he was disappointed in the first issue of the magazine. "The good features of *First Statement* and *Preview* are not too apparent and nothing in it was startling or very remarkable" (UT, Spring 1946). For a time it seemed as if a new Toronto magazine *Reading* might act as a competitive impetus for

Northern Review, but *Reading* ceased publication in 1946 after a few issues. Raymond Souster closed down *Direction* too in 1946 after ten sporadic issues. Souster's magazine had been more of a wartime newsletter than a little magazine and had run from November 1943 to February 1946. It did seem in this immediate post-war period that the little magazine movement was losing impetus.

With the October 1946 number, *Contemporary Verse* completed "five years of hazardous progress" (19:16). It had outlived both *Preview* and *First Statement*, in spite of the "isolation" of the west and Crawley's "handicap," but five years of "hazardous progress" maintaining the high standard that was the trademark of *Contemporary Verse* had taken a toll, and Crawley considered merging with *Canadian Poetry Magazine* when Earle Birney took over as editor in the fall of 1946. There would be advantages. With the financial backing of the Canadian Authors' Association, *Contemporary Verse* could be expanded and printed (Crawley's one great regret regarding *Contemporary Verse* was that he never managed to get the magazine printed—in this he envied *First Statement* and *Northern Review*). Crawley would be relieved of some of the editorial responsibilities, and he and Birney were compatible and would probably make a good team. On the other hand, *Contemporary Verse* was well established as a modern poetry magazine of high quality and Crawley as an astute and honest critic. The traditionalism and mediocrity of the Canadian Authors' Association might destroy this hard won reputation and with it the usefulness of the magazine. Crawley tried the idea of a merger out on a number of *Contemporary Verse* poets, and P.K. Page's adamant letter is typical of their responses. Page firmly supported Birney: "*If* Birney does take this on I will back him because I feel if the C.A.A. has enough wits to appoint him editor they deserve whatsoever help we can give"; but she felt Birney should take over *Canadian Poetry Magazine* on his own and not jeopardize *Contemporary Verse*. "Also," Page concluded, "I *personally* like to feel CV is there—small and compact, reflecting you" (AC, nd). F.R. Scott agreed: "How are you making out with Birney and his schemes? No idea of dropping CV I trust. You have your own supporters and your own place among the poetry magazines and it would be a pity to cease publishing now" (AC, 16 Feb. 1947). Crawley decided against the merger and Earle Birney took over *Canadian Poetry Magazine* on his own. Now with the Montreal coterie magazines defunct and three liberal magazines active (and spread across Canada in Vancouver, Toronto, and Montreal), eclecticism was the dominant mood in Canada.[7]

Earle Birney commanding the Canadian Authors' Association garrison was an astonishing happening for modern poetry in Canada. Just as astonishing was Alan Crawley's cross-Canada poetry "saying" tour in the late fall of 1946. It was an enormous boost for Crawley and for modern poetry. In ten weeks Crawley spoke to more than fifty large and enthusiastic audiences from

Vancouver to Montreal. Not since Bliss Carman's triumphal reading tours of the 1920's had Canadian audiences had a chance to hear live presentations of contemporary poetry. Crawley had an excellent voice for saying poetry—clear and capable of a great range of nuances and moods—and an excellent repertoire of contemporary work alive and ready in his memory. The pace of the tour was hectic. Crawley wrote to Birney that he had "demanded a day and a night for ourselves" in each of Ottawa and Montreal following "the three weeks of one night stands, five days a week in Ontario" (UT, nd). He used basically the same format for these "sayings" that he had worked out the preceding spring for a series of poetry talks for local and university audiences in Vancouver. He challenged his hearers with the statement: "I have to understand the poems to say them and if they make sense to me they will to you" (19:19). Then he proceeded with his sayings interspersed with down-to-earth comment on the poems and sometimes a bit of biographical information about the poet if it seemed relevant to the poem. He described an early talk to Earle Birney:

> Started to talk at eight twenty and said the last telling words at ten to ten so they had a belly full. It really went well and I was for a wonder a bit pleased. . . there was great attention and I felt the audience of some eighty or so was thoroughly interested and taking it all in. Dorothy [Livesay] and Pat Page said it went well and even my critical Jean was pleased. (UT, nd)

Birney was excited and positive about Crawley's talks. "The big and positive audiences you got, in spite of hellish weather, proves that people will listen to poetry if only the poets will write in a way that can be listened to and will get out on a stage or in front of a mike and yell a little, and give support to people like yourself, who read it in public as it should be read" (AC, 4 April 1946). It is impossible to assess the impact Crawley's saying tour had on the general public—Crawley had jokingly written to Birney, "Tell me if there is any jump in your sales, or god help me, any falling off" (UT, nd)—but it was a great help to Crawley and *Contemporary Verse*. The tour gave Crawley a chance to meet and talk to most of the poets and people connected with writing and publishing across Canada. Crawley knew many of these people through their letters, but it was not the same as meeting and talking to them face-to-face. He came back to Vancouver stimulated by the exchange of news and ideas, even more enthusiastic about poetry, and bolstered by the promise of manuscripts from a number of poets. He approached the editing of *Contemporary Verse* with renewed vigour in 1947.

Stimulated by the vitality of this period and still chafing at A.J.M. Smith's classification of modern Canadian poetry into the "native" or the ''cosmopolitan'' stream in the *Book of Canadian Poetry*, John Sutherland prepared his own anthology—*Other Canadians: An Anthology of the New Poetry in Canada, 1940-1946*—with its argumentative, irritating, perspicacious introduction, and unimaginative selection of poems. A.M. Klein was indignant at Sutherland's anthology and complained about it to Crawley:

> I do not think much of Sutherland's book. That the volume contains some good poems is, of course, not his fault. They were written by others. But the literary standards, the lack of logic and the sheer malice which characterizes the introduction, makes one rage where it does not make one laugh. (AC, 5 Sept. 1947)

Crawley was more tolerant of *Other Canadians* in his review of it in the summer 1947 issue of *Contemporary Verse*. He recognized the inadequacies of the selection of verse (including the fact that all eighteen poets represented lived east of Manitoba), but he felt the introduction was important and stated why:

> These important things are: his clever analysis of ''national'' and ''colonial'' influences on Canadian poetry; his estimation of the poetry, past, present, and future; the timely and deserved appraisal of the poetry of Louis Dudek and Raymond Souster and the repeated evidence of Mr. Sutherland's sensitive feeling and enthusiasm for contemporary poetry. (21:18)

Sutherland was grateful for Crawley's reasoned assessment and wrote ''I liked the review of Other Canadians, which seemed to me very fair as well as penetrating. It was by all odds the most intelligent comment of any reviewer on the quality of the introduction'' (AC, 4 April 1948). Sutherland had expected *Other Canadians* to be a corrective to the *Book of Canadian Poetry* and perhaps to the course of modern poetry in Canada; instead it was a postscript to a period. Canadian poetry was moving into a new phase.

CHAPTER THREE

New Departures: *Contemporary Verse* 1947-1952

> How suddenly it all changed! The First Statement Press had no sooner published *Other Canadians: An Anthology of the New Poetry in Canada, 1940-1946*, which I furnished with a bristling, defiant introduction, than the whole purpose and driving spirit of the "new movement" were in a state of decay. We had barely rushed to the side of this challenger of tradition, holding up his right—or rather his left—hand in the stance of victory, when the challenger laid his head upon the block and willingly submitted to having it removed.[1]

The war was over and life settled into a comfortable mediocrity. Canadians returned gratefully to middle-class values of materialism, social prestige, and security. It left the poets who rode the crest of the war beached and silent. Earle Birney wrote to Alan Crawley early in 1946:

> I really mean it about future verse-writing. The new mag., "Reading," has two of mine in its first issue but they are ones you already saw; I have written no more. If ever I get out of the CBC and back into the life of the semi-leisured classes, I will try prose; but to produce anything else in this Philistine paradise is a waste of spirit and expense of shame. (AC, 20 Feb.)

The eastern writers felt discouraged too. From Frank Scott:

> Your visit [while Crawley was on tour] was the last time we had so many of the local writers together. Even our Northern Review meetings these days are getting scrappy—and so perhaps is N.R. The core seems to have

> gone. Perhaps Patrick Anderson was it, and he lives out of town. (AC, 16 Feb. 1947)

But in the west coast office of *Contemporary Verse* there was still enthusiasm in the spring of 1947. The contacts Crawley made during his saying tour in 1946 resulted in a rich assortment of manuscripts. There was fresh and promising work from new poets and sharp finished poetry from the seasoned writers. The spring issue carried James Reaney's "School Globe," his second appearance in *Contemporary Verse*, and Livesay's "Page One." The next few issues brought more of Reaney, a first meeting with Anne Wilkinson, a rare glimpse of Malcolm Lowry, and sound work from P.K. Page (including "Puppets" and "The Permanent Tourists") and A.M. Klein ("O God! O Montreal" and "Monsieur Gaston"). Scott, Smith, Souster, Dudek, Birney, Roy Daniells, and L.A. MacKay contributed too. Floris McLaren had a new, bolder cover designed for the magazine, and Crawley increased the number of pages—first to twenty, then twenty-four, and occasionally an issue was made up with twenty-eight pages. The publishing houses (notably Ryerson, Macmillan, and McClelland and Stewart) regularly bought advertising which covered the cost of printing the covers, and the circulation of *Contemporary Verse* increased to three hundred.

The flavour of *Contemporary Verse* is different after the war. The "common attitude" that Smith talked about in the *Book of Canadian Poetry* "which unites all the very different individual poets into a single recognizable school" is gone and so is the bulk of didactic, social realist poetry.[2] There is more variety and gaiety, and there are more love poems. There is fantasy, symbol, and myth; there are poems about moths, words, hats, eating lunch in Rockcliff Park, a school teacher in November, and Bartok and a geranium. It is not that the poems are not serious; the intricacies of life are not avoided, neither are the joys. But the reader of post-war forties' poetry is less likely to be instructed and more likely to be entertained than the earlier reader. Seventy-seven poets published three hundred and ten poems in *Contemporary Verse* between 1947 and 1952. The transition poets left the magazine except for an occasional appearance. Floris McLaren's poem "Mountaineer," in the summer 1948 issue, is a moving epitaph for those poets who seemed permanently caught between the romantic and modern traditions:

> He reaches each lookout just as the others leave
> Accepts the view with no discoverer's eye
> Conscientiously reading the locked sky,
> The rivers looped in Sanskrit;
> But is moved to solitary tenderness
> By hair-stemmed twinflower,
> The minutely separate lacquer cups of moss. (25:6)

Anne Wilkinson, James Reaney, and P.K. Page have the most poems in *Contemporary Verse* during this period; followed closely by Louis Dudek, Jay Macpherson, and Raymond Souster; and distantly by Colleen Thibaudeau, Miriam Waddington, F.R. Scott, and Kay Smith. Dorothy Livesay and Earle Birney command substantial space with fewer but longer poems—"Call My People Home" and selections from "Damnation of Vancouver."

Alan Crawley had a surprising ability to attract and recognize new talent, especially in this second half of the forties when poetry moved in new directions and poets became more individualistic. James Reaney's poetry was first published in *Contemporary Verse* and so were the first poems of Jay Macpherson and Daryl Hine. Others—Anne Wilkinson, Margaret Avison, Phyllis Webb, J.K. Heath (a promising poet killed in the Korean War), Elizabeth Brewster, and Marya Fiamengo—were recognized early in their poetic careers and published and encouraged by Crawley. "I envy you your knack of catching all the promising younger poets before the rest of us know they exist" (AC), John Sutherland wrote to Crawley in June 1949. Sutherland had just read the spring issue of *Contemporary Verse* which featured six of Jay Macpherson's poems. They were her first work and she was seventeen.

James Reaney, who first appeared in 1946, took the entire literary tradition and the Canadian experience as his canvas; and if his early poems are sometimes derivative and contrived, they are never dull. John Sutherland saw Reaney as a corrective for Canadian poetry. "What we can do to combat the indifference with which C.V. and Northern Review still meet, I do not know, unless James Reaney sets us the example," Sutherland said in a letter to Crawley early in 1948:

> I have been delighted to see him trundling along at the heels of Canadian poetry, coloured like a zebra escaped from a circus, and uttering that amazing horse-laugh of his. There is something really appropriate about that laughter, as if he had taken in the whole cavalcade ahead of him at one glance, and that is why his horse-laugh is really horse-sense. I find that reading Reaney is a good way of warning off Northern Review. (AC, nd)

Evocations of childhood experiences, but not contrived or sentimental ones, dominate Reaney's early poems, as in "Childhood Musette." He nonchalantly combines the exotic, the literary, and the everyday with a savoir faire uncommon in Canadian poetry. His poetry (unlike most of the early forties' poetry and much from after the war) is unselfconscious, and even when nostalgic or macabre, it contains an eagerness and a zest for life. He happily clusters the incompatible—"Intestinal paths" and a "vicious fox" with a face "like a bicycle seat"—in the lush "The Rape of the Somnambulist":

Into a thicket where tumble
And noctambulate
Luna-moths whose eyes resemble
Tears in a sunset
In a thicket of Jack-in-the-pulpit,
Each green preacher a hypocrite,
She softly descends.... (23:10)

But Reaney can speak plainly too, as he does in "Miss Newport's Letters":

Miss Newport is moving,
In her garden she burns
All her correspondence. (18:11)

James Reaney was a twenty-year-old student at the University of Toronto when he submitted his poems to *Contemporary Verse*. "They're rather unfinished and awful, but I am so anxious that you should see my work" (AC, 27 Sept. 1946). Reaney asked for a chance to meet Crawley when he was in Toronto on his saying tour to discuss his poetry further. Later after *The Red Heart* had been published, he thanked Crawley "for all the encouragement and assistance I've got from you and C.V."; and commented, "I can still remember how ecstatic I was when you first accepted a poem of mine; and the ecstasy still has not died out" (AC, 10 Dec. 1949).

Another new poet, Anne Wilkinson, first appeared in *Contemporary Verse* at the same time. Considerably older than Reaney—Anne Wilkinson was thirty-six in 1946—she had only recently begun writing poetry seriously and had had little published. In a sense Wilkinson and Reaney were opposites in their poetic development. Reaney had considerable technical virtuosity, but his sensibility was still essentially unformed. On the other hand, Anne Wilkinson showed maturity in even her earliest poems, but lacked craftsmanship. She had not yet found the way to translate her particular vision of life, and much of the poetry she submitted to *Contemporary Verse* was sent back for revision or for complete rewriting. The Crawley-Wilkinson correspondence between 1946 and 1951 shows the kind of careful and supportive criticism that Crawley gave to writers during his years of editing *Contemporary Verse*.

Crawley met Anne Wilkinson in Toronto when he was on tour. She told him she was writing poems (a few had been published in *Reading*) but was uncertain of their quality and hesitated to submit them to editors. He offered to read them and late in December 1946 a whole book of Wilkinson manuscripts arrived. Crawley was delighted:

Last night for the first time I opened the book of your poems and you can

> have no idea of the delight and exhilaration I had in reading the MSS. It is such a rare thing for me to find such freshness and vitality and originality of expression and I do thank you very deeply for letting me have the reading. There are so many of the poems I would like to have for C.V. that I would be a glutton, the list mounts as I go over them a second time. (UT)

He chose two poems for *Contemporary Verse* 18, eight for the next number (these issues appeared much later than their stated dates of July and October 1946), and six for number 22 including "Theme and Variations," "Momism," and "Pastoral." A.J.M. Smith was particularly impressed with *Contemporary Verse* 22 and wrote: "The new CV has just come in—a swell number made so by Klein and Wilkinson" (AC, 7 Jan. 1948).

"Pastoral," which Wilkinson left out of her first book, *Counterpoint to Sleep*, but added to her later collection, *The Hangman Ties the Holly*, evolved after extensive reworking. Crawley was "very struck" with "Pastoral" at first reading, but felt that it was really three separate poems at that point. He suggested separating them and dropping part three which was "too loose and does not quite come off":

> I have felt in the few of your longer poems I have seen that you are apt to lose the thread of the thought and do not keep strictly to this all through the poem. This of course is a very common tendency and particularly among the younger writers. When it is overcome and the main idea is the sole theme the poem becomes forceful and memorable and it is much easier for the writer to control form. (AC, 5 Sept. 1947)

Wilkinson agreed with Crawley "on every point re Pastoral. Your letter was the greatest stimulant imaginable. I am starved for criticism. I never see anyone who reads my poetry and you can have no idea of the value your letter has for me," she wrote.

> When I put the three under one title I had my doubts at the time—it was more because I wrote them simultaneously than for any logical reason that I felt they were one poem. It was the last thing I had written when I sent it off and my usual practice is to consider nothing finished until I have buried it for three months, dug it up and revised it. As long as I am writing something I'm in love with it and the judgement only comes after the burial when the corpse is brought back to daylight and seen with the indifferent eyes of an ex lover. (AC, 15 Oct. 1947)

"I am writing a longish poem called 'After reading Kafka's The Trial' but I am afraid to show it to anyone,'' Wilkinson wrote on 30 November 1947 (AC). Crawley replied: ''please believe that I would like to see any MSS if you think there is a chance I might be able to help you with it in any way, even if you do not want to let me have it for C.V.'' (UT, nd). The manuscript arrived with Wilkinson's letter of 9 December 1947:

> I think it is bad (the poem not the book!), perhaps excruciatingly bad but until someone tells me so, bluntly, I'll go on trying to make something of it instead of turning to new work. I not only esteem your criticism but act on it and if you say ''forget Kafka,'' I'll at least forget this particular effort without too much sorrow. (AC)

Crawley liked the poem ''the deeper I go into it.... There is a great deal of thought packed into its good images and lines but it could be better...it seems to me incomplete and needs some further fashioning on the wheel.'' He worked through the poem concentrating mainly on fuzzy syntax and on individual lines that needed clarifying or strengthening. ''Do not lay this away,'' he encouraged, ''It is too good to be left'' (UT, 7 Feb. 1948). Wilkinson's letter of 10 March 1948 brought word that she was working on the poem again—''Everything you told me about it has helped enormously'' (AC)—and the revised poem was in Crawley's hands by May. Still it did not suit him, and he returned it with suggestions for further revision; it was ''greatly improved and strengthened,'' but not yet finished (UT, nd). When it came back, reworked and with a new title ''After Reading Kafka,'' Crawley was satisfied and published the poem in the summer 1948 issue of *Contemporary Verse*.

Crawley was a generous editor, willing to put a writer's personal development ahead of his own need to gather up enough copy to make an issue of *Contemporary Verse*. He advised Anne Wilkinson to submit a group of her poems to *Poetry* (Chicago)—including the Kafka poem on which he had worked so hard—in order to get her work better known. ''Not,'' he said, ''that I think Poetry is always all-hell in its grandeur but it has come to represent some desired achievement'' (UT, 29 Oct. 1948). She was at a loss to know which poems to select and how to group them most effectively, so Crawley did it for her and submitted the manuscripts as well. *Poetry* sent them back, but *Here and Now* and *Canadian Forum* accepted some.

Anne Wilkinson's ability to know when a poem was finished and if it was good was slow in developing. The quality of her manuscripts was as mixed and her letters were almost as uncertain in the 1950's as they had been five years earlier. The group of three poems in the summer 1950 issue of *Contemporary Verse*—''Summer Acres,'' ''Winter Sketch,'' and ''Folk Tale: With a Warning to Lovers''—were part of a large batch of poems she had submitted to

Crawley in the spring. Crawley thought these three showed "a great deal of progress in your work, in construction, development, imagery, and in adherence to your thought and scheme....'Winter Sketch' and 'Summer Acres' are the best and most complete work you have done," Crawley wrote; and "'Folk Tale' did amuse me and gave me a good deal of pleasure." The others were mediocre. "None of them moved me emotionally or to thought, speculation or remembering"; they were bits and pieces, "more cerebral than vigorous and affecting" (UT, nd). A year later Crawley returned a batch of poems saying they lacked tension, point, and vitality. He advised Wilkinson to "attack and use more variety in poetic form, taking a hurl at traditional patterns and mastering their rigidity.... You have the talent and ability," Crawley scolded, "it now requires that application and discipline and hard work without which the napkin can never be completely withdrawn" (UT, nd). He felt that Wilkinson's heavy schedule of reading—she had written recently that she was writing little but reading voraciously and "studying Greek and full of excitement about it" (AC, 12 Nov. 1950)—was taking her away from her native poetic roots. Your recent poems "are in many parts genuine Anne Wilkinson," Crawley wrote, but "they are less important to Canadian writing than are those poems which have essential 'Canadian ingredients'":

> You know that I am not a bigoted booster for national or regional writing yet I do feel that it is helpful if writers who have a wide knowledge and close and deep intimacy with Canadian life and surroundings make use of this as much as possible for the good of their writing and of our creative life. (UT, nd)

In August 1952, Wilkinson submitted her long poem "Letter to My Children" to *Contemporary Verse*, and Crawley accepted it gladly, relieved that her slump was over:

> I like the long poem it is real AW work in every way and much better than the others you sent me some months ago. Of course I want it but I think you should first send it to Poetry Chicago. It might be what they would take yet if they do not some comments from them might be helpful and you must keep trying.... If they don't take it, and golly I hope they do for you should be in that magazine, do not dare to let John have it but send it back to me for the next CV at the end of the year. (UT, 16 Aug. 1952)

Another important new poet Alan Crawley worked with was Jay Macpherson, corresponding with her for almost two years before any of her poems appeared in *Contemporary Verse*. Every letter is laced with encouragement, aimed at sustaining this very young poet's self-esteem and commitment to writing (Macpherson was fifteen when the correspondence began):

> I am certain I shall have considerable exhilaration in keeping up with your work (JM, 21 May 1947)
> You have packed, most expertly and finely a great deal into a few lines in each poem. That is poetic skill. (JM, 8 Feb. 1949)
> When work which shows such promise and talent as yours comes unexpectedly, there is exhilaration and compensation that is unbelievable unless it is experienced. (JM, 16 March 1949)

Crawley told Anne Wilkinson that "Jay Macpherson is rather an amazing and a bit frightening young women":

> She is not yet eighteen and at college in Ottawa and for some time has been sending me MSS. strictly marked not to be published and including some poems written in English, French and German and translations that is translations of poems written originally in either of those back and forth into and from one of the others. . . . I believe that if she is able to hold her balance and to find something that she really wants to say and can say it she will do something worthwhile. (UT, nd)

By the spring of 1949, Jay Macpherson felt ready to appear before a larger audience. Six of her poems are in the twenty-seventh issue of *Contemporary Verse*, and they show Macpherson at this early stage—even before her association with Northrop Frye—already a symbolic, mythopoeic poet and already exploring the themes that have become central to her work. "Ordinary People in the Last Days" introduces the unicorn symbol which figured prominently in *The Boatman* collection:

> The unicorn yielded to my sweetheart.
> She was giggling with some girls
> When the unicorn walked carefully up to her
> And laid his head in her lap. (27:7)

Several of the poems use water/sea imagery and symbolism, including "Seasons" and "Seascape," which introduces the religious theme central to Macpherson's work—the struggle for grace—a theme picked up and explored in the "poor child" image and myth of "Objective Correlative: Poor Child." The "poor child" image informs several later poems in *Contemporary Verse* ("The Comforter," "The Comforted," and "Ill Wind"); and Macpherson uses it as the controlling idea in the first section of *The Boatman*.

Alan Crawley felt that the inclusion of Jay Macpherson's six poems in *Contemporary Verse* 27 was a significant happening in Canadian literature. He soon had other opinions to back him up. Dorothy Livesay wrote: "CV spring number was a grand surprise. What a fine haul you made with the poems by Jay Macpherson. I was greatly excited with them. Who is he?" (JM, 27 May 1949). Anne Wilkinson hurried off a note: "C.V. arrived this morning. On a rapid first reading I find the poems by Jay Macpherson remarkably exciting—particularly the first—but more about C.V. after a careful reading" (AC, 25 May 1949). Ira Dilworth (then head of the Canadian Broadcasting Corporation International Service) sent a letter: "My copy of Contemporary Verse has just come.... The poems of Jay Macpherson are most interesting. If Contemporary Verse published nothing else than these I should be quite satisfied with my subscription" (JM, 27 May 1949). "I have not had before so many references to any contributor's work in so short a time since publication and I feel very pleased and proud and rather possessive," Crawley confided to Macpherson (JM, 27 May 1949). He later wrote that "No. 27 will be a collector's piece, already we have few of it left for complete files" (JM, 14 July 1949).

In her allusiveness and use of (often literary) myth and symbol Macpherson is somewhat like Reaney. Desmond Pacey remarked on their similarities in his "Literature of the Fifties" addition to *Creative Writing in Canada*. He assigned them to his "mythopoeic school" (Wilkinson is there too) and noted Macpherson's resemblance to Reaney "in wit, allusiveness and intricacy of technique"; but finds Macpherson a "more elegant and reserved poet."[3] Macpherson worried about the allusive quality of her poems, but Crawley reassured her:

> Referring to one of your questions about allusions in your poetry which might escape the reader...I do not find your poems obscure, rather stimulating and evocative. You use...few private or obscure images and so though your writing is not direct, it is not intentionally obscure. (JM, 16 March 1949)

Allusive, symbolic, mythological; the multilevelled richness of Anne Wilkinson's, Jay Macpherson's, and James Reaney's poetry signalled a new departure for *Contemporary Verse* and for Canadian poetry in the years 1947 to 1952.

But there was good work from the established poets too, though P.K. Page's poetry stands out from the rest of her early forties' contemporaries. Alan Crawley had thought in 1946 that Page's collection *As Ten As Twenty* was chiefly important as a demonstration "that Miss Page has the equipment of a poet and the ability to use this"; but that "it is not so evident that she has yet found the theme or absorbing interest which will enable her to make fullest use of that endowment'' (19:17). P.K. Page was never comfortable with the strong political orientation of the other *Preview* writers, and after the war, essentially on her own with her poetry, she quickly perfected the precise, intense, introspective poetry that became characteristic of her—''The Permanent Tourists,'' ''Photographs of a Salt Mine,'' ''Puppets,'' ''Portrait of Marina.'' Technically Page's poems in the post-war *Contemporary Verse* (most of them would be collected in *The Metal and the Flower*) show a marked increase in skill. She has mastered her tones, her diction is more exact and more vivid, and her ability to create a controlling image and modulate it into new shapes and nuances is superb. In ''Photographs of a Salt Mine'' the poem moves in a series of photographs from salt-snow whiteness and purity to the black inferno of guilt. Curiously, Page was uncertain of the quality of these very accomplished poems: ''I am very self-conscious about all the stuff I've written in the last year [1950-51] and quite honestly cannot tell whether it should all be burned or not. Perhaps it should and my feelings will not be hurt if you say so. But I would like some idea of the stuff'' (AC, nd). Crawley was satisfied that they were good poems; but Irving Layton did not agree. Renewing his subscription to *Contemporary Verse* (''as an act of faith and optimism''), he commented on number 35:

> Page's poems are sloppy and disappointing in the extreme. Now that there seems to be no concern with technique, only the feverishness remains. In the entire issue there is not a line or a phrase that is recallable; everything is blurred, misty, full of damp crawling things. (FMcL, nd)

The poetry of Louis Dudek and Raymond Souster continued in essentially the same lyric vein. They each had a large group of poems in the twenty-third issue which seem all the more personal and lyric in company with James Reaney's mythopoeic group. Dudek's explanatory letter to Crawley is as pertinent to Souster's selection as to his own:

> Your selection pleases me because it is in the direction which I like at present. It is the kind of lyric which is most characteristic of my work. I am trying to give as purely as possible the experience which is pure and isolated in my mind, and which is the imaginative image of the poem. (23:21)

Dudek contributed regularly to *Contemporary Verse*, but until his final selection in the summer 1952 issue of the magazine, there was no indication that his poetry was moving in new directions. In that issue two of his poems ''Words, Words, Words'' and ''The Function of Criticism (in Our Time),'' are concerned with the nature of poetry itself; and both are uncharacteristically turgid. Souster has fewer poems in the later issues of *Contemporary Verse*, and none at all from early 1948 through 1951. He submitted poetry regularly, but Crawley did not feel it was up to standard and rejected it. Souster's five poems in the winter-spring 1952 issue are obvious and hackneyed, but they were better than some he had submitted and Crawley was having difficulty filling *Contemporary Verse* with really good work. Souster had written to Crawley a year earlier about his poetry in a tone of frustrated exasperation: "I am in a stage of transition right now in my poetry, and have not yet found the road which I want to travel ahead on. It is easy for the critic to expect the poet to develop, much harder for the poet to carry out the idea" (AC, 31 March 1950).

Dorothy Livesay and Earle Birney experimented with new verse forms in the late forties and early fifties—Livesay with the greater success. Her documentary poem, "Call My People Home," is aligned to her thirties' poems "Day and Night" and "The Outrider"; but it is longer, more ambitious, and has an added dramatic dimension through being written for broadcast. It is more lyric than the earlier documentary poems, subtler and more controlled, openly emotional without being sentimental:

> As we set sail at midnight, now a thousand boats
> Chained to the naval escort, steadily south
> Into familiar waters where the forests cooled their feet
> At rocks end, mountains swam in mist—
> As we set sail for home, the young ones, born here, swore
> Not softly, into the hissing night. The old men wept. (28:7)

Earle Birney's verse drama "Damnation of Vancouver" is a more ambitious undertaking, and more literary and scholarly. But Birney fails to universalize the experience of the poem, and the alliance of a slangy contemporary city life, native lore, and medieval English history is uneasy. In "Damnation of Vancouver," Birney attempts to do in large what he did so brilliantly on a small scale in "Anglosaxon Street."

Livesay's other poetry in *Contemporary Verse* shows a sure increase in lyric power and intensity—"Ancestral Theme," "Page One," "Bartok and the Geranium"—while Birney's shows a perceptible decline. "I am in many minds about E.B. and his late work which seems to me often marred and sullied by a strange new quirk though he does have a fine architectural sense and some good lines," Crawley remarked anxiously to A.J.M. Smith (UT, 10 Jan. 1948).

The late forties' poetry in *Contemporary Verse* (as well as that from the first year or two of the fifties) is cooler and more personal than that of the earlier years. The anger, indignation, and political panaceas of the earlier poetry are gone and so (largely) is the gaucheness. The emphasis on specifics and the here-and-now of the "aggressively realistic poetry of early modernism"[4] has given way to more universal concerns—the search for enduring patterns of myth, religion, the cycles of nature which would give coherence and meaning to life. But the search was not a comfortable one. In this mood L.A. MacKay wrote to Crawley:

> I wish I could offer effective support in some more literate fashion than a cheque, but the vein seems to have pinched off. Perhaps poetry is necessarily the by-product of maladjustment, in some way or another, and I am just too content to write, too much at ease in Zion. (AC, 2 Aug. 1951)

Dudek saw this move away from aggressive realism as in bad faith. He argued the point with Crawley as he commented on Raymond Souster's retrospective article for *Impression* on the early forties' movement:

> I agree with him that our little boom was a late echo of the Auden-Spender line. And After? We need to realize just how much of a sense of hopeless crisis there now is. . . and how much of a retreat into the internal world, safe corners, logorrhoea, romanticism (none of these acceptable to *us*) has taken place in the face of this hopelessness. And refuse to lie down and die. (AC, 23 Feb. 1952)

For Alan Crawley and *Contemporary Verse*, 1946 and 1947 were peak years. The magazine had already won its reputation as the best poetry magazine in Canada, and Crawley was regarded as the most discriminating editor; there was exciting new work from young writers, a comfortable margin of subscribers, and there were Crawley's public lectures, informal talks, and radio broadcasts on poetry. All this was satisfying but exhausting; and in the late fall Crawley confessed to Anne Wilkinson that "this year after the forty or so talks on the Canadian Club tour and some additional lectures on poetry here early in the year I have gone 'stale' on poetry and could not work up any enthusiasm over a fresh project and this state of mind is discouraging and unhealthy" (UT, nd). During the summer of 1947, the slump that F.R. Scott had talked about in his February letter had spread west. The summer "has been desperately barren of new work" and "the standard has been so low, in what I have had sent me," Crawley continued in the same letter, "that *Contemporary Verse* has had to sit idly waiting. This dry condition has affected all the publications using poetry here in Canada and so far the fall has not done much to remedy."

The "dry condition" worsened in 1948. Crawley was hard pressed to scrape enough material together to warrant publishing *Contemporary Verse*—and it shows in the magazine. Issue 24 is particularly uncharacteristic with its mixed-bag of single poems instead of the usual satisfying groups of poems. "It must be quite a battle to keep CV going," F.R. Scott wrote, "but I hope you will never be too discouraged":

> This apathy you speak of is all over this country, thick and heavy like a sheet of glue. What makes it? No pep anywhere, hence little art. Or is it no art, hence little pep? Anyway you are doing a fine job in maintaining a plot of ground on which the spirit may walk freely, and breathe the upper air. (AC, 23 Oct. 1948)

A.J.M. Smith's revised *Book of Canadian Poetry* brought a little stir of activity to 1948. Smith wrote to Crawley in early January asking for "comments and advice" on his proposed changes; and Crawley, in general, concurred with them. But Crawley thought that Kay Smith should not be included—"she has done some good things but too few and so many of them are messy and the promise she gave seems failing and she does not write, after all it is a poet's business to be a poet"—and that Anne Wilkinson and James Reaney should. Reaney, Crawley wrote, "is doing a lot of work and is a worker and his stuff is completely different from that of any other contemporary" (UT, 10 Jan. 1948). Posterity has proved Crawley's judgement right. Smith ended his segregation of the modern writers in the revised edition and thus ended the native-cosmopolitan controversy. He grouped the moderns together and commented:

> The five years that have elapsed since the publication of the first edition of this book have been unusually rich in the production of modern Canadian verse by a talented group of writers, who seem to have escaped from the limitations of provincialism into a cosmopolitanism that does not reject native sources of strength but draws nourishment from them.[5]

When the Massey Royal Commission on National Development in the Arts, Letters and Sciences started work in 1949, Crawley presented a brief, hoping for more substantial returns than "interest." He suggested that the best way to encourage writers was to provide adequate publication outlets and to pay them for their work. It was a sore point with him that throughout the twelve years of *Contemporary Verse* he was never able to pay contributors—not even the token amount that Sutherland managed with *First Statement* and *Northern Review*—nor to print his magazine.

Poets gave their full support to Crawley and *Contemporary Verse*; but, as with most Royal Commissions, there were no benefits immediate enough to help the magazine. What writers said about *Contemporary Verse* shows how important the magazine was to them and to Canadian poetry during the forties. Jay Macpherson wrote that "I know very well that I. . . should never have ventured into print last spring if it had not been for your continual encouragement" (AC, Sept. 1949). "Take Contemporary Verse out of the Canadian literary scene and you have nothing left west of Longitude 85' " (AC, 1 Sept. 1949), said James Reaney. Anne Wilkinson wrote simply "I for one am continuing to write poetry because there is a Contemporary Verse. . . . The United States has a hundred good outlets for the poet; Canada has one. Contemporary Verse holds together Canadian poetry" (AC, Sept. 1949). Roy Daniells thought that *Contemporary Verse* "has consistently attracted the best of the established poets and at the same time given space to promising unknown writers—no mean feat. Its standards of admission have been high, and what is equally important, they have been consistent. The ups and downs of other periodicals are in striking contrast" (AC, 5 Sept. 1949). And Earle Birney remarked:

> In my opinion Alan Crawley's *Contemporary Verse* has given the most valuable service to poetry of any Canadian publication in the last decade. It is the only Canadian verse magazine which has consistently maintained high editorial standards. It has introduced a number of important younger Canadian writers to the public and encouraged them to continue writing. What space it has been able to give to criticism has been intelligently used. The whole tone of the magazine has been literary, responsible, and stimulating. (AC, Sept. 1949)

In 1950 Alan Crawley tried to interest Canadian poets in an anthology of new, unpublished work. "I have roughly thought of a book somewhat the form of Unit of 5 which would give each writer 78-81 lines, a single poem of 24 lines to a page. This is of course an elastic estimate and allotment" (UT, nd), he explained to Earle Birney. Poets were interested in the idea of an anthology, but few had the new work to submit. Some, like P.K. Page, were reluctant to give a publisher prior rights over a fair amount of work.

> In view of the fact that on the whole Canadian writers are not overly prolific such a stipulation (all new work) might leave you with a much poorer selection than you think. Also I think, speaking for myself, the idea of having 84 lines tied up for so long a time—for book publication is slow—is rather depressing.

Yet in spite of her objections, Page was willing to support the project with "the best I have to offer. . . . Certainly CV should have some kind of a between hard covers aspect to it—for it has maintained a consistently high standard now for an astonishingly long time" (AC, 28 Nov. 1950). But Crawley had to abandon the idea. He wrote to Birney that "there was a lot of encouraging approval of the plan and of my trying it, but far too many of the writers I must have wrote that they had no unpublished work and so that is that" (UT, nd). It was 1941 all over again; an editor asking poets for work and poets coming up empty-handed. In 1952 Crawley tried once more to edit an anthology—this time of significant and representative work from *Contemporary Verse*—but publishing difficulties scotched the plan.

In 1949 and 1950 the pattern of groups of poems returns in *Contemporary Verse*, and such newcomers as George Woodcock, Wilfred Watson, Norman Newton, and J.K. Heath make an interesting contrast to the regular contributors. Some of the older poets reappear (for some it is a first appearance)—F.R. Scott, Roy Daniells, A.M. Klein, Alfred G. Bailey—seeming very substantial beside unknowns who disappear after one or two contributions. Several issues stand out—number 28 for Dorothy Livesay's "Call My People Home" and Crawley's "Notes on A.M. Klein"; number 29 for John Sutherland's little known analysis of Northrop Frye's "Canada and Its Poetry"; number 32 for Dudek's article "A Visit to Ezra Pound" and for good poetry by Wilkinson, Klein, Scott, and Bailey.

In the fall of 1951 *Contemporary Verse* completed ten years of publication. Alan Crawley reassembled the original contributors (supplemented by E.J. Pratt, F.R. Scott, L.A. MacKay, Anne Wilkinson, and J.K. Heath) for the anniversary issue. The issue was nostalgic. The members of the founding committee—Doris Ferne and Anne Marriott—and business manager Floris McLaren had been absent from the magazine (except for one or two poems) since the war years; and Leo Kennedy and L.A. MacKay had left Canada and had given up writing. Their offerings here were acts of friendship more than of creativity. The presence of Canada's three senior poets adds weight and solemnity. Scott's "Last Rites" takes the honours for the issue. Pratt's contribution, "Cycles," is his only appearance in *Contemporary Verse*. Smith seldom published during this period, and Birney's and Page's poems are not of their best work. Crawley wrote a foreword—"C.V. 1941-1951"—which he intended to be a retrospective glance at a decade of publishing and editing but which turned out to be an expression of his own doubt and uncertainty about the future of the magazine:

> During this summer and up to a few weeks ago I have been wavering and distrustful of my decisions; even though the hundreds of manuscripts which have been sent to me for approval for publication and the many letters which have come to Floris McLaren and to me convince me that CV has given help and encouragement to many young writers, that there is still a need for this work to go on, and that much of what we hoped would and could be done by CV has been accomplished.

His concluding statement that *Contemporary Verse* will continue—"the place occupied by Contemporary Verse has not yet above it a sign TO LET"—is not entirely convincing. "There is a job for CV in presenting the best of Canadian poetry written in the 1950's as it has presented that of the last ten years," Crawley wrote. "If such poetry is written, then so long as it is possible, Floris McLaren and I will get out CV in very irregular order and with as great interest and pride in what we are doing as we have done for 36 times" (36:4).

Crawley's uncertainty reflected a general lack of direction in Canadian poetry in the early fifties, as Robert Weaver noted in his *Critic* review of *Contemporary Verse* and its decade of publishing: "When Mr. Crawley feels uncertain of himself and of the function of his magazine at the present time, it seems to me that he is simply reflecting the uncertainties of Canadian poetry during a period of change."[6] Certainly, magazine publication had been erratic during the late forties, and things seemed to be worse in the early fifties. There simply was not the creative impetus to keep magazines going. Earle Birney resigned from *Canadian Poetry Magazine* in June 1948, discouraged at the lack of good poetry available and disgusted at the narrowness and mediocrity of the Canadian Authors' Association; and *Here and Now*, the most impressive magazine in format that Canadians had seen, came and went in only four issues. Several other little magazines made brief appearances—*PM* (from Vancouver), *Impression* (from Winnipeg), *Protocol* (from Newfoundland)—but did not last long enough to make an impression. In spite of John Sutherland's herculean efforts, *Northern Review* was never on firm ground, poetically or financially. Sutherland got out two issues in 1948, four in 1949, six (which is what he was aiming for) in 1950 and in 1951, but only three in 1952. His growing conservatism alienated Dudek, Layton, and Souster who had been his main support since the *Preview* poets left the magazine in 1947. Crawley commented on the precarious position of *Northern Review* and on Sutherland's changed editorial policy in a letter on 27 June 1950 to Anne Wilkinson:

> I hear from many quarters that John Sutherland is predicting a wind up of Northern Review if he cannot get together a sum sufficient to carry on for another year. I am sorry to hear this as he has done a good work though the magazine since last summer has, it seems to me, got into a less interesting and less important manner and J.S. appears to be stressing patriotism and regionalism a bit too far. I can never get wildly excited at an urging to praise Canadian products of any kind just because they come from Canada. In spite of this I admire John and his amazing energy and doggedness. (UT)

The discouragement that Crawley expressed in his foreword to the anniversary issue of *Contemporary Verse* roused an immediate response in

Canadian poets. If *Contemporary Verse* closed down, the ailing *Northern Review* would be the only periodical left to support poetry writing. The Montreal poets were so alarmed they sent a telegram to Crawley:[7]

> Montreal poets meeting tonight are convinced survival Contemporary Verse essential to Canadian literature stop Your ten years prove value of little magazine encouraging new and established writers to publishing best work stop You must present the fifties as you have presented the forties. (AC, 15 Oct. 1951)

And soon after came an enthusiastic, rallying letter from Dudek:

> Impossible to think of the literary scene and Contemporary Verse not there. I would not believe it. That telegram from F.R. Scott's house came with or went with a true concern for CV and a desire to make you realize how important we think it is. A few hundred readers? Say it were ten. Ten may be the node of life in the midst of an organism, one of the small life cells. Enough! Literature is that important.

Literature is the "one outpost holding out" in "this disease of modern life," Dudek said, and "one has no right to give up. . . . Who knows if we won't have better poetry in the fifties than (even) the forties. Let's all be around for the birth pangs" (AC, 13 Nov. 1951). L.A. MacKay said simply that "the disappearance of CV would leave a horrid gap in Canadian letters. I have no confidence that a new team would take over; the country would probably be left to the glories of CPM, except for the very mixed fare of the CF, seldom very tasty, and the scant commons of NR" (AC, 2 Aug. 1951).

The praise encouraged Crawley: but a magazine cannot run on praise. He hoped poets would support their good wishes with manuscripts, and some did, but not enough. Crawley got number 37 out (late) by doubling up winter and spring into one issue. The summer 1952 issue of *Contemporary Verse* (also late) would have been thin without Birney's eight pages of selections from "Damnation of Vancouver." In July Crawley wrote to Jay Macpherson who was then in England:

> All writing in Canada this year dreadfully dull and depressing, lifeless and grinding out old stuff or new work no value. . . . CV in a pretty deplorable state at the moment, a better bank showing than ever before and with not enough MSS to make another issue. No one is writing PK, Reaney, Thibeaudeau, Avison doing no poetry or prose or hack work. I am very disheartened and think seriously that CV has no further work to do, certainly not for the present. If a need comes again there will be someone and some magazine to fill it. (JM, 5 July 1952)

The fall number of *Contemporary Verse* was delayed, then delayed again into the winter of 1952 as Crawley waited for good material to come in. Abruptly, in February 1953, he gathered up the material he had, assembled it with the notice that the magazine was closing, and sent out number 39—the final issue of *Contemporary Verse*. The decision to close down the magazine was neither "sudden" nor "capricious," Crawley wrote; it was made "after much consideration and is weighted with regret at the termination of eleven years of an absorbing job. . . . We have a strong belief that the work of a little magazine under the same editor's direction declines in time from its peak of usefulness. In this conviction we close our files and write the abrupt and final statement that this is the last issue of CV" (39:1). Dorothy Livesay, close to Alan Crawley and *Contemporary Verse* from the beginning, agreed with—but rued—Crawley's belief that he was no longer doing a good job (or as good a job) as editor. Her letter of 16 February 1953 reacting to the close of *Contemporary Verse* is angry, honest, and supporting. "I had sort of thought, having been so definitely a midwife, I might have been called in at the death," she began:

> I am sad, but not to cry. Where there is no enthusiasm, poetry perishes. And I have felt strongly, this past year, that you have lost the fiery interest you once had. For this we are all probably to blame—we writers, that is. We move on and where we move does not perhaps interest you. I mean, you have to think of the publication and how it stands up; we think only of our own development; we have to have faith in ourselves and our direction. And your frequently expressed sense of disappointment—because work is not the same as it was—does incline one to question: why should it be? How could it be?
>
> No: if you were to carry on you would have to depend not on the older generation who started the works, but on young men like Daryl; and if there were enough of them around I would urge you to continue. But I suppose there aren't!

"In any case," she closed, "nothing has been lost: all the effort was to the good and terribly worthwhile; and the start you gave so many will always be bearing fruit—even if from trees that will not nourish you! Others will be nourished" (AC).

CHAPTER FOUR

Conclusion

The passing of *Contemporary Verse*, as L.A. MacKay had prophesied, left a "horrid gap," and writers and readers immediately realized it. "Nothing can quite take its place," F.R. Scott wrote, but "of one thing you can be sure: through it you have become part of the literary history of Canada, and you have the gratitude of a whole generation of poets. . . . I have some unpublished poems to send out somewhere," Scott went on, "now where shall I turn?" (AC, 8 March 1953). Jay Macpherson wrote demanding that Crawley "continue to make your influence felt. . . . You can't *leave* the field to the doggerel-obscenity-mongers" (AC, 20 March 1953). Dudek's letter is full of regret. "I gather from your letter that nothing can be done to save CV. It is a great pity, since you've got such a fine record behind you, and there is the need of a mag on the West Coast. However, however...I guess somebody else will get busy eventually" (AC, 10 March 1953).

The Canadian publishers realized, perhaps better than anyone else, how important a bridge between poetry writing and book publication a magazine such as *Contemporary Verse* was—setting standards, offering criticism, trying the work out on the public. Jack McClelland wrote to Alan Crawley:

> It was a shock and a disappointment to learn that Contemporary Verse is no longer to be published. It has served a fine purpose in the last ten years and I can think of no one who has made a greater contribution to Canadian letters than you have done through the publication of this magazine. . . . It is a matter of sincere regret to me that we have not done a good deal more to actively support the publication through the years. (AC, 26 March 1953)

Lorne Pierce from Ryerson was more personal:

> I shall miss CV more than I can say. It was consistently good as a magazine, and kept the banner of integrity blowing bravely in the breeze. But most of all it spoke of you, a very gracious and a very gallant gentleman. I am thankful for all you have done for Canadian letters, and for your kindness to me. (AC, 14 April 1953)

Like so many others who wrote at this time, Dudek felt that he should have given more help to Crawley and *Contemporary Verse*:

> I think I've never done enough for CV. Lack of brains on my part (I'm always oppressed with a sense of my *lack of intellect* as compared with other so-called intellectuals) has kept me in all sorts of muggy ruts, especially in poetry, and the good things I write have been too scarce, too hard to pick out from the trash (especially before revision), maybe have gone to the wrong magazines.... Bad emotions interfere with my intellection and memory; that's where I envy the others. In any case, CV has meant a lot to me, gave me a start almost from the beginning, and the correspondence in the New York years helped get a few things off my chest and keep confidence going. (AC, 10 March 1953)

Manuscripts from poets would have helped Crawley, but it was not only the lack of material that prompted him to close *Contemporary Verse* in the winter of 1953. For the preceding year or two, Crawley had been "wavering and distrustful" of his decisions about poetry, as he wrote in the anniversary number (36:4). He felt that the creativity that produced the "renaissance" of the forties was dying away. A new impetus and new directions were needed. Margaret Avison described the effect of this vacuum on her poetry writing in a letter to Crawley on 14 June 1952. She talks of distractions, discouragement, and "no focus point":

> I feel rotten about the frittering I seem to do earning a living, reading maybe too much and too rapidly, writing first drafts of poems now and then, when little pools of quiet occur, and then never going back to polish as they require. And never putting the loose pages of them in order or keeping track of what should be salvaged, what would come out after enough working over, what should be thrown away and forgotten. It is a state of confusion and unseemliness that grows worse with time.... (AC)

Crawley sensed that Canadian poetry was moving in a direction he was not in step with. If he could not be sensitive to new moods in poetry, if he could not accept the new poetry on its own terms, and began instead to dictate what poetry should be, then he was no longer useful as an editor. These were his feelings when he wrote to Anne Wilkinson on 4 November 1952:

> I feel very strongly that a little magazine has its place and its work but that both are ended when the cycle of its immediate usefulness appears to have run its course and this feeling is one that has come to all who have started and carried on and ended one of those magazines. The work done in Canada and published in the last two or three years has not been up to the standard of that done in the late forties, and I am not relying only on what has come to me in MSS but on that and what I have seen in other magazines. Also I feel that perhaps I have stayed behind in criticism and appreciation of what the young writers are now trying to do and so am not able to give as much help and useful criticism as I was able to give twelve years ago. (UT)

Possibly the appearance of Souster's little magazine *Contact* encouraged Crawley's questions about his own editorial abilities. By 1951 Souster was disgruntled enough with *Northern Review* and *Contemporary Verse* to start a new magazine—one that would be international in flavour and open to what he felt were vital influences from the United States. He was aided by Dudek who wrote to Crawley 13 November 1951:

> Souster will crank out Contact soon a new mimeo magazine. No matter how many copies will come out, it will be a welcome noise they'll make. Souster has the kind of irrascibility that one expects from an honest mind in these times. The Apollonian will come to him late, if ever. (AC)

Crawley felt sad that Souster had not told him of his plans—he wrote to Wilkinson "I had a letter from Souster less than three weeks ago in which he did not mention the plan and I feel a bit hurt that after many years of letters between us and what I thought was some sort of friendship that he had not told me of what he was up to"—but wished him well:

> I really feel that it is a good sign that there is some feeling among the younger writers that they want their own publications, just as there was in the early forties, that these, no matter how long they last, are enlivening and a good thing and do something to awaken interest in reading and stimulate writers. (UT, nd)

The first issue of *Contact* appeared in January 1952, introducing Canadians to the work of Cid Corman, Charles Olson, and Robert Creeley. It was the beginning of a new period for Canadian poetry.

Canadian poets, on the whole, were critical of Souster's new magazine. Jay Macpherson, for example, condemned it on aesthetic grounds in a letter to Crawley. She commented on the translations of Gottfried Benn("apparently quite unauthorized") which "are *bad*: he really is a decent poet, though one would hardly have guessed it," then went on:

> Mother feels it's a pity the feeling aroused in Mr. Layton by "the Girls of his Graduating Class" couldn't be brought to the attention of Quebec Home and School Ass'n. As for Mr. Dudek, who appears to think that every minute during which young ladies are not sleeping with young gentlemen is wasted, even at high noon—no comment. However, compared to some of their authors, the restraint of these two seems commendable.—My objection isn't that the stuff isn't decent, it's that it's not poetry: anything's decent if handled with sufficient love, intelligence, sensitivity, and discipline. (AC, 18 Nov. 1952)

Anne Wilkinson wrote to Crawley that "I am not sorry that I withdrew" from *Contact* (AC, 20 March 1952). John Sutherland frankly disliked the magazine from the start. Souster "is lacking in any sense of critical values, as he is in a sense of editorial responsibility, and I think if the magazine had much currency—which, fortunately, it won't—it would be a real setback to all our efforts to develop a more intelligent attitude in Canada towards the writing of poetry" (AC, 12 March 1952). Dudek sounded a bit defensive about *Contact* in his 23 February 1952 letter to Crawley:

> I think Souster's CONTACT should do some good as it gets going and makes its critical point clear. So far people . . . students etc. . . . have asked "What's the idea? What is it supposed to be trying to do?" It's the kind of noise that's necessary in the very correct drawing room atmosphere of Canadian poetry at the moment. (AC)

Crawley himself was undecided about *Contact*. He did not really like the magazine, but it had a certain energy that made it seem worth reading. In March 1952, Crawley wrote to Wilkinson that "I have seen the two numbers of Contact and am not very excited over them, the introduction by Dudek has not so far been fulfilled by what has been printed. . . . Whether Souster can improve and discipline his critical ability remains to be seen, he is still gripped by the enthusiasms and crusades of adolescence" (UT). In June he discussed the magazine with Wilkinson again. "What to think of Contact fuddles me and I hold off. Messers Dudek, Souster and Layton may set some broth boiling in their combined efforts promised by Contact Press." It could be that *Contact* might act as a catalyst to start new activity in poetry—"most of what I get lately does little to start me crowing but there may be new life ready to spring up somewhere" (UT, 4 June 1952).

Alan Crawley was a forties' man. He grew up on modern poetry from England and the United States, and he was on hand, an enthusiastic welcomer and supporter, when modernism settled in Canada in the forties and took over Canadian poetry. Crawley was one of the main sponsors of this new poetry through his magazine *Contemporary Verse*, and no one worked harder than he to help get it naturalized in Canada. But just as he was sensitive to the beginning of this trend in 1941, he recognized its ending in the early years of the fifties and chose to close down his magazine with the termination of this distinctive period in Canadian poetry. He believed, as he wrote in the final number of *Contemporary Verse*, "that the work of a little magazine under the same editor's direction declines in time from its peak of usefulness" (39:1). In the fifties, there was need for new directions, new vigour, and new editors. "I do not read a great deal of contemporary poetry," Crawley said in 1969, "I find that. . .I don't get as much satisfaction or pleasure out of it as I do out of reading the poems that I knew or by writers that I have known some years ago."[1] It took courage and a firm hand to close *Contemporary Verse*; twelve years earlier it had taken the same kind of courage and firmness to begin it.

The militant manifestoes, calls to arms, and polemic criticism which *First Statement* (and *Preview*) provided raise blood pressures and interest and get people moving; but in the long run change comes about through the slow process of growth and maturation. The first requirement is a place to grow, and *Contemporary Verse* provided that. It was the first of the forties' little magazines; it lasted the longest, and it consistently maintained high standards.

"It was the function. . .of Little Mags like *Contemporary Verse, Preview, First Statement* and *Direction* to subvert the prevailing literary values of a lingering genteel Romanticism and to establish Modern poetry in Canada," Wynne Francis wrote in her article on little magazines in Canada.[2] The policy making and proselytizing of *Preview* and *First Statement* were essential to the establishment of modernism in Canada; just as essential were the high standards and eclecticism of *Contemporary Verse*, which encouraged a poet to do his best and to realize his own individuality. Dudek criticized *Contemporary Verse* in 1958 for not being a "fighting magazine with policy";[3] but in a more recent letter he has changed his mind and sees the value of the magazine's eclecticism as a necessary balance to the cliques and partisanship which dominated early forties' poetry. "Alan Crawley stood in a sense above the battle, outside the partisanship of *Preview* and *First Statement*, and outside political partisanship. His magazine was a cool place and we were all able to appear in it together" (JMcC, 7 July 1970).

If Alan Crawley is known at all it is through *Contemporary Verse* and, perhaps, through his radio discussions and public poetry "sayings." His extensive work as critic, adviser, and confidant of many of the major poets of the forties is seldom discussed. Crawley probably preferred it so, for he was a quiet and unassuming man, his satisfaction came from doing the work, not from seeing his accomplishments chronicled in literary history. But the extra-editorial work that Crawley did had a significant impact on individual poets and on the development of poetry during the forties. "No one knowing you through the magazine alone could ever guess at the giant behind the scenes job you do," P.K. Page said in a letter to Crawley in 1951. "I feel sorry that you have to suffer for your virtues—but this faculty you have which is that of the good psychiatrist! is to make your 'patient' feel he can show you anything he has written. It is more important to the writer than CV is even, and that, heaven knows is important enough" (AC, nd).

Crawley had a rare ability to see the way a poet was going and help him move in that direction without imposing his own views and preferences. Crawley's interest and letters bridged the isolation many poets felt. He was the best possible audience—sensitive, enthusiastic, and honest. Without Crawley's guidance and encouragement, it is unlikely that Anne Wilkinson would have progressed far beyond occasional magazine publication. "I've had this material ready to send you for some time but have been so preoccupied with domestic affairs that I had almost forgotten that I used to try and write verse," Wilkinson wrote in May 1949.

> I'm enclosing a new version of Morning Song with the old one so that you can compare them. I wrote the revised verses immediately on receiving your stimulating words of criticism. I'd write more if I lived in the atmosphere of interest and criticism that you create, so miraculously, in your letters. (AC)

P.K. Page, Floris McLaren, Earle Birney, Anne Marriott, Dorothy Livesay, James Reaney, Jay Macpherson—all of these poets counted on Crawley's creative criticism and support. So did Souster—"Thanks for the criticism you have given me, straight from the shoulder. Some of it has been a little hard to take, but I believe it has done me good" (AC, 31 March 1950)—and Dudek, who said:

> *Contemporary Verse* meant a great deal to me in my New York years (I lived there from 1944 to 1950, unless Mike Gnarowski corrects the dates).... I wrote to Alan, as I remember, as to a kind of father-confessor; you must remember that in those days magazines were fewer—I myself was a beginning writer—and we were grateful for any editor's attention and a chance of publication.

Dudek is unusual in that he did feel that Crawley tried to shape his poetry in a way that impeded his development as a poet, "I think I sent him some bad poetry and maybe he published some of it," he reminisced in the same letter. "As I recall, he wanted me to write lovely innocent lyrics of the sort I wrote at the very beginning. But I felt I was going toward something more real and more complex, and that it was a mistake to try to recall a writer to his past" (JMcC, 7 July 1970). A very young Daryl Hine phoned Crawley one day and asked to come and talk about poetry—"He was just about 15 and he had a sheaf of manuscript in his hand; we went down to my room and he read to me for about two hours, most remarkable writing for a boy of that age."[4] Later on Hine submitted some work to *Contemporary Verse*; Crawley suggested some changes and Hine replied—respectful but hurt and possessive:

> I was interested to hear that you wished to discuss the Dedicated Poem further, with me. I am curious about what particular points in the poem you feel need revision. I hope that faults which detract from what I feel to be the basically sound construction of that poem may be remedied. (AC, 11 March 1952)

Five years later, with his first collection of poems ready for the press, Daryl Hine sent Crawley a warmly grateful letter:

> I don't believe that I ever told you how much your encouragement meant to me five years ago, when I first visited you in West Vancouver. I had been writing then for about two or three years, but I doubt that I should have persevered through the vicissitudes of adolescence had you not been so kind and so perceptive. Certainly I left you that day resolved at any rate to continue my attempts for another few years to prove whether or not I was, in reality, a poet. (AC, 20 Dec. 1956)

It is the kind of letter that makes an enormous amount of work worthwhile. Crawley received many like it.

In the last issue of his magazine, Crawley wrote: "The story of CV through its more than a decade of publication is already written in the 39 issues since Sept. 1941. Once again, reading these issues, I am proud of the overall excellence of the poetry published there which has made, for CV and for the writers, an assured and high place in the history of Canadian writing" (39:27). It is a fitting epitaph for the magazine that was so large a part of and presents so graphically the "renaissance" of the forties.

Notes

NOTES TO THE FOREWORD

1. George Robertson, "Alan Crawley and Contemporary Verse," *Canadian Literature* 41 (Summer 1969): 89-96.
2. J.E. Rea, *Winnipeg General Strike*, Canadian History through the Press Series (Toronto: Holt, Rinehart and Winston, 1973).
3. A.R.M. Lower, *My First Seventy-Five Years* (Toronto: Macmillan, 1967), p. 171.

NOTES TO THE INTRODUCTION

1. Louis Dudek and Michael Gnarowski, eds., *The Making of Modern Poetry in Canada* (1967; rpt. Toronto: McGraw-Hill, 1970), p. 113.
2. Louis Dudek, "The Montreal Poets," *Culture* 18 (1957), rpt. in *The McGill Movement*, ed. Peter Stevens (Toronto: Ryerson Press, 1969), p. 6.
3. Louis Dudek, "Patterns of Recent Canadian Poetry," *Culture* 19 (1958), rpt. in *Making of Modern Poetry*, pp. 276-78.
4. Munro Beattie, "Poetry, 1920-1935," in *Literary History of Canada*, ed. Carl F. Klinck (Toronto: University of Toronto Press, 1965), pp. 730-31.
5. Beattie, "Poetry 1950-1960," ibid., p. 766.
6. Desmond Pacey, *Creative Writing in Canada*, 2nd ed., rev. (Toronto: Ryerson Press, 1961), p. 142.
7. Ibid., p. 154.
8. Earle Birney, "A.J.M.S.," *Canadian Literature* 15 (Winter 1963):4.
9. Wynne Francis, "The Montreal Poets," *Canadian Literature* 14 (Autumn 1962): 23.
10. Pacey, *Creative Writing in Canada*, p. 154.
11. All further citations of letters will be included in the body of the text immediately following the quotation. The following information will be given: initials of the holder of the letter, the writer and receiver of the letter, and the date of the letter. When part or all of the preceding information is included in the text it will be excluded from the citation.
12. Beattie, "Poetry 1950-1960," p. 766.
13. Dudek and Gnarowski. *Making of Modern Poetry*, p. 113.
14. Ibid., p. 204.
15. Louis Dudek, "The Role of Little Magazines in Canada," *Canadian*

Forum 37, (July 1958), rpt. in Dudek & Gnarowski, *Making of Modern Poetry*, p. 208.

16. Floris McLaren, ''Contemporary Verse: A Canadian Quarterly,'' *Tamarack Review* 3 (Spring 1957): 55-63.
17. Ethel Wilson, ''Of Alan Crawley,'' *Canadian Literature* 19 (Winter 1964): 33-42.
18. George Robertson, ''Alan Crawley,'' p. 89-96.
19. Michael Gnarowski, ''The Role of Little Magazines in the Development of Poetry in English Montreal,'' *Culture* 24 (1963), rpt. in Dudek & Gnarowski, *Making of Modern Poetry*, p. 222.
20. F.R. Scott, ''Preface,'' *New Provinces* (Toronto: Macmillan, 1936), p.v.
21. A.J.M. Smith, ''A Rejected Preface,'' *Canadian Literature* 24 (Spring 1965): 8.
22. Ibid., p. 9.
23. Peter Stevens, ''The Development of Canadian Poetry between the Wars and Its Reflection of Social Awareness'' (Ph.D. diss., University of Saskatchewan, 1968), p. 165.
24. E.J. Pratt, ed., *Canadian Poetry Magazine* 1, no. 2 (April 1938): 6.
25. Leo Kennedy, ''Direction for Canadian Poets,'' *New Frontier* 1, no. 3 (June 1936): 24.
26. Ibid., pp. 21, 22-23.
27. F.R. Scott, *New Provinces,* p.v.
28. W.E. Collin, *The White Savannahs* (Toronto: Macmillan, 1936), p. 158.
29. Alan Calmer, ''A Hope for Canadian Poetry,'' *New Frontier* 1, no. 6 (October 1936): 29.
30. E.J. Pratt, ''Canadian Poetry—Past and Present,'' *University of Toronto Quarterly* 8 (October 1938): 8.
31. A.J.M. Smith, ''Canadian Poetry—A Minority Report,'' *University of Toronto Quarterly* 8 (January 1939): 135-36.
32. E.K. Brown ''The Development of Poetry in Canada, 1880-1940,'' *Poetry* 58 (April 1941): 47.

NOTES TO CHAPTER ONE

1. John Sutherland, ''The Past Decade in Canadian Poetry,'' *Northern Review* 4, no. 2 (December 1950—January 1951), rpt. in Dudek & Gnarowski, *Making of Modern Poetry*, pp. 118-19.
2. Ibid., pp. 116-17.
3. Citations of material quoted from *Contemporary Verse* will in included in the body of the text in parenthesis immediately following the quotation. Information given will be: first the issue number, second the page

number. For example, a quotation from the first issue, second page would be cited (1:2).

4. P.K. Page, "Canadian Poetry, 1942," *Preview* 8 (October 1942): 8. P.K. Page was troubled about the review and wrote to Crawley: "You were generous about my article. I no sooner saw it in print that I wished to disown it—and send out letters to everyone saying 'there has been a mistake.' Actually I still agree on the whole with what I said but it was so condensed that it seemed distorted. And the fact that I was a Previewer and a would-be poet seemed to make it worse—as if I were setting myself above everyone else, which I was not doing" (AC, n.d.).
5. Floris McLaren, "Contemporary Verse," p. 55.
6. Ibid.
7. E.K. Brown, "Letters in Canada: 1941," *University of Toronto Quarterly* 11 (1942): 294.
8. McLaren, "Contemporary Verse," pp. 56-57.
9. Ibid., p. 57.
10. Ibid.
11. George Robertson, "Alan Crawley," pp. 88-89
12. Northrop Frye, (Review), *Canadian Forum* 21 (December 1941): 283.
13. E.J. Pratt, *Canadian Poetry Magazine* 6, no. 1 (December 1941): 46.
14. Earle Birney, *Canadian Forum* 22 (April 1942): 29.
15. James Reaney, "Editorial," *Alphabet*, no. 16 (September 1969): 2-3.
16. Robertson, "Alan Crawley," p. 87.
17. "Statement," *Preview* 1 (March 1942): 1.
18. *First Statement* 1, p. 1
19. *First Statement* 3, p. 1
20. Robertson, "Alan Crawley," p. 92.

NOTES TO CHAPTER TWO

1. A.J.M. Smith, *Book of Canadian Poetry* (Toronto: W.J. Gage and Co., 1948), p. 32.
2. Ibid.
3. Birney wrote back that "the line you find harsh was more or less, intended to be so, i.e. the inversion throwing the emphasis on 'blood', is deliberate. I wanted the words to cause a small shock, at the moment. I can see that the inversion may be too ugly, however" (AC, 20 Feb. 1943).
4. Patrick Anderson, P.K. Page, F.R. Scott, Bruce Ruddick, Neufville Shaw, and later A.M. Klein.
5. Raymond Souster, "Poetry Canada, 1940-1945," *Impression* 1, no. 4 (Spring 1952): 69.

6. There were three issues of *Northern Review* in 1946, four in 1947, two in 1948.
7. *Fiddlehead* from New Brunswick was still strongly oriented to keeping the Carman-Roberts tradition alive.

NOTES TO CHAPTER THREE

1. Sutherland, ''The Past Decade,'' p. 119.
2. Smith, *Book of Canadian Poetry*, p. 32.
3. Pacey, *Creative Writing in Canada*, p. 238.
4. Dudek and Gnarowski, *Making of Modern Poetry*, p. 114.
5. Smith, *Book of Canadian Poetry*, p. vii.
6. Robert Weaver, ''Books,'' *Critic* 2, no. 2. (February 1952): 6.
7. It was signed by A.M. Klein, Louis Dudek, F.R. Scott, John Sutherland, Audrey Aikman, Phyllis Webb, and Neufville Shaw.

NOTES TO CHAPTER FOUR

1. Robertson, ''Alan Crawley,'' p. 94.
2. Wynne Francis, ''Literary Underground: Little Magazines in Canada,'' *Canadian Literature* 34 (August 1967): 68.
3. Dudek, ''Little Magazines in Canada,'' p. 208.
4. Robertson, ''Alan Crawley,'' p. 94.

Bibliography

Primary Sources

LETTERS

Alan Crawley (holder): letters written by Margaret Avison, A.G Bailey, Earle Birney, Roy Daniells, Louis Dudek, John Gray, Daryl Hine, A.E. Johnson, George Johnston, A.M. Klein, Dorothy Livesay, Malcolm Lowry, Jack McClelland, L.A. MacKay, Jay Macpherson, P.K. Page, Lorne Pierce, E.J. Pratt, James Reaney, W.W.E. Ross, Duncan C. Scott, F.R. Scott, A.J.M. Smith, Raymond Souster, John Sutherland, Wilfred Watson, Phyllis Webb, and Anne Wilkinson to Alan Crawley.

Joan McCullagh (holder): letters written by Louis Dudek, Daryl Hine, Irving Layton, L.A. MacKay, Jay Macpherson, James Reaney, Mary E. Ross, F.R. Scott, A.J.M. Smith, Raymond Souster, Lionel Stevenson, and A.G. Wilkinson to Joan McCullagh.

Floris McLaren (holder): letters written by Alan Crawley, Irving Layton, Lionel Stevenson, and Robert Weaver to Floris McLaren.

Jay Macpherson (holder): letters written by Alan Crawley to Jay Macpherson.

University of Toronto (holder): letters written by Alan Crawley to Earle Birney, A.J.M. Smith, and Anne Wilkinson.

ANTHOLOGIES AND INDIVIDUAL COLLECTIONS OF POETRY

Bennett, Ethel Hume, ed. *New Harvesting*. Toronto: Macmillan, 1939.

Benson, Nathaniel A., ed. *Modern Canadian Poetry*. Ottawa: Graphic Publishers, 1930.

Carman, Bliss; Pierce, Lorne; Rhodenizer, V.B., comps. *Canadian Poetry in English*. Toronto: Ryerson, 1954.

Creighton, Alan, and Ridley, Hilda M., eds. *A New Canadian Anthology*. Toronto: Crucible Press, 1938.

Gustafson, Ralph, ed. *Anthology of Canadian Poetry*. Harmondsworth: Penguin Books, 1942.

Hambleton, Ronald, ed. *Unit of Five*. Toronto: Ryerson, 1944.

Kennedy, Leo. *The Shrouding*. Toronto: Macmillan, 1933.

Knister, Raymond. *The Collected Poems of Raymond Knister: With a Memoir.* Edited by Dorothy Livesay, Toronto: Ryerson, 1949.

Livesay, Dorothy. *Green Pitcher.* Toronto: Macmillan, 1928.

———. *Signpost.* Toronto: Macmillan, 1932.

MacKay, L.A. *Viper's Bugloss.* Toronto: Ryerson, 1938.

McLaren, Floris Clark. *Frozen Fire.* Toronto: Macmillan, 1937.

Marriott, Anne. *The Wind Our Enemy.* Toronto: Ryerson, 1939.

New Provinces: Poems By Several Authors. Toronto: Macmillan, 1936.

Pratt, E.J. *Collected Poems.* Toronto: Macmillan, 1962.

———. *Many Moods.* Toronto: Macmillan, 1932.

———. *The Witches Brew.* London: Selwyn & Blount, 1925.

Ross, W.W.E. *Shapes and Sounds: Poems by W.W.E. Ross.* Edited by Raymond Souster and John Robert Colombo. Toronto: Longmans 1968.

Smith, A.J.M., ed. *The Book of Canadian Poetry.* 1943. Rev. ed. Toronto: W.J. Gage, 1948

———, ed. *Collected Poems of Anne Wilkinson.* Toronto: Macmillan, 1968.

Sutherland, John, ed. *Other Canadians: An Anthology of the New Poetry in Canada, 1940-1946.* Montreal: First Statement Press, McClelland & Stewart, 1947.

Wilson, Milton, ed. *Poetry of Mid-Century 1940-1960.* Toronto: McClelland & Stewart, 1964.

Secondary Sources

Bernhardt, Clara. "The Poet's Function." *Canadian Poetry* 4 (December 1939): 5-10.

Birney, Earle. "A.J.M.S." *Canadian Literature* 15 (Winter 1963): 4-6 .

Boylan, Charles Robert. "The Social and Lyric Voices of Dorothy Livesay." M.A. thesis, University of British Columbia, 1969.

Brown, E.K. "The Development of Poetry in Canada, 1880-1940." *Poetry* (Chicago) 58 (April 1944): 34-47.

Collin, W.E. *The White Savannahs.* Toronto: Macmillan, 1936.

Cramer, Alan. "A Hope For Canadian Poetry." *New Frontier* (October 1936): 29.

Dehler, Charles Ronald. "Canada's English Poetry Since Thirty-Nine" *Culture* 14 (Summer 1953): 247-55.

Djwa, Sandra Ann. "Metaphor, World View and the Continuity of Canadian Poetry: A Study of the Major English Canadian Poets with a Computer Concordance to Metaphor." Ph.D. dissertation, University of British Columbia, 1968.

Dudek, Louis, and Gnarowski, Michael, eds. *The Making of Modern Poetry in Canada: Essential Articles in Contemporary Canadian Poetry in English*. Toronto: Ryerson, 1967.

———. "Patterns of Recent Canadian Poetry." *Culture* 19 (Winter 1958): 399-445.

Francis, Wynne. "Literary Underground: Little Magazines in Canada." *Canadian Literature* 34 (Autumn 1967): 63-70.

———. "The Montreal Poets." *Canadian Literature* 14 (Autumn 1962): 21-34.

Gnarowski, Michael. *Contact 1952-1954: Notes on the History and Background of the Periodical and an Index*. Montreal: Delta Canada, 1966.

Harder, Helga Irene. "English-Canadian Poetry 1935-1955: A Thematic Study." M.A. thesis, University of British Columbia, 1965.

Kennedy, Leo. "A Direction For Canadian Poets." *New Frontier* 1 (June 1936): 21-24.

Klinck, Carl F., ed. *Literary History of Canada: Canadian Literature in English*. Toronto: University of Toronto Press, 1965.

McLaren, Floris Clark. "Contemporary Verse: A Canadian Quarterly." *Tamarack Review* 3 (Spring 1957): 55-63.

Macnair, Dorothy Livesay. "Rhythm and Sound in Contemporary Canadian Poetry." M.Ed. thesis, University of British Columbia, 1966.

Mandel, Eli. *Contexts of Canadian Criticism*. Chicago: University of Chicago Press, 1971.

Meis, Joanne Elizabeth. "Little Magazines and Canadian War Poetry 1939-1945; With Some Reference to Poetry of the First World War." M.A. thesis, University of British Columbia, 1971.

Pacey, Desmond. *Creative Writing in Canada*. Rev. ed. Toronto: Ryerson, 1967.

———. *Essays in Canadian Criticism 1938-1968*. Toronto: Ryerson, 1969.

———. *Ten Canadian Poets: A Group of Biographical and Critical Essays*. Toronto: Ryerson, 1958.

Pratt, E.J. "Canadian Poetry—Past and Present." *University of Toronto Quarterly* 8 (October 1938): 1-10.

Rashley, R.E. *Poetry in Canada: The First Three Steps*. Toronto: Ryerson, 1958.

———. "Editorial." *Alphabet* 16 (September 1969): 2-3.

Ringrose, Christopher Xerxes. "'Preview': Anatomy of a Group." M.A. thesis, University of Alberta, 1969.

Robertson, George, ed. "Alan Crawley and Contemporary Verse." *Canadian Literature* 41 (Summer 1969): 89-96.

Roskolenko, Harry. "Post-War Poetry in Canada." *Here and Now* 2 (June 1949): 31-37.

Smith, A.J.M. "Canadian Poetry—A Minority Report." *University of Toronto Quarterly* 8 (January 1939): 125-38.

——, ed. *Masks of Poetry: Canadian Critics on Canadian Verse*. Toronto: McClelland & Stewart, 1962.

——. "A Rejected Preface." *Canadian Literature* 24 (Spring 1965): 6-9.

Souster, Raymond. "Poetry Canada, 1940-45." *Impression* 1 (Spring 1952): 67-69.

Stevens, Peter. "The Development of Canadian Poetry between the Wars and Its Reflection of Social Awareness." Ph.D. dissertation, University of Saskatchewan, 1968.

——, ed. *The McGill Movement: A.J.M. Smith, F.R. Scott and Leo Kennedy*. Toronto: Ryerson, 1969.

Weaver, Robert. "Books." *Critic* 2 (February 1952): 5-6.

Wilson, Ethel. "Of Alan Crawley." *Canadian Literature* 19 (Winter 1964): 33-42.

Contemporary Verse
1941-1952
Index

When *Contemporary Verse* began, the issues were designated by both volume and number (Vol.1, nos. 1-4 and Vol. 2,no.5); thereafter they carried the issue number only (6-39). The dates of the issues were as follows: 1, September 1941; 2, December 1941; 3, March 1942; 4, June 1942; 5, September 1942; 6, December 1942; 7, March 1943; 8, June-September 1943; 9, January 1944; 10, April 1944; 11, July 1944; 12, January 1945; 13, April 1945; 14, July 1945; 15, October 1945; 16, January 1946; 17, April 1946; 18, July 1946; 19, October 1946; 20, Spring 1947; 21, Summer 1947; 22, Fall 1947; 23, Winter 1947-48; 24, Spring 1948; 25, Summer 1948; 26, Fall 1948; 27, Winter-Spring 1948-49; 28, Summer 1949; 29, Fall 1949; 30, Winter 1949-50; 31, Spring 1950; 32, Summer 1950; 33, Fall-Winter 1950; 34, Spring 1951; 35, Summer 1951; 36, Fall 1951; 37, Winter-Spring 1951-52; 38, Summer 1952; 39, Fall-Winter 1952.

DIRECTIONS FOR USE

The Index has been arranged in one alphabet to include all author entries, title entries, and such subject headings as have been considered necessary. In reference to an individual entry, the number of the issue is given first, and the page or pages of the entry follow.

A

B

I

N

O

P

Q

T

U

V

W

Index